YOUR NAME

YOUR NUMBER

YOUR DESTINY

YOUR NAME

YOUR NUMBER

YOUR DESTINY

―――――――――

TWO GUIDES TO NUMEROLOGY

BY

HELEN HOUSTON

AND

JUNO JORDAN

―――――――――

Introduction by Dorothy B. Hughes

NEWCASTLE PUBLISHING CO., INC.

NORTH HOLLYWOOD, CALIFORNIA

1982

Contents

Introduction

We are surrounded by numbers in our modern world as a means of identifying us and our place here. Most of us have telephone numbers, a house number, driver's license or I.D. number, a credit card number, a Social Security number, a bank account number, a license number for our car, etc., etc. Did it ever occur to you that there might be a deeper meaning to those numbers than appears on the surface?

Alexis Carrel, in his book *Man, the Unknown* (Harper & Bros., 1935), has said: "Man should be the measure of all. On the contrary, he is a stranger in the world that he has created. He has been incapable of organizing this world for himself because he did not possess a practical knowledge of his own nature. . . . The only possible remedy for this . . . is a much more profound knowledge of ourselves. Such a knowledge will enable us to understand by what mechanisms modern existence affects our consciousness and our body."

While Alexis Carrel was speaking largely from the standpoint of physical science, he was conscious also of the avenues of metaphysical thought, though this was not the thrust of his book. It is fine to wish to explore the physical aspect of man, but the questions confronting many people today are not those which can be answered by physical science.

Either early or late in life, almost every person will face these questions: "Who am I?" "Why am I here?" "What can I do with my life?" "How will I attain my best expression?" In this world of our Creator, by whatever name we call Him, there is a place and a need for each person or that person would not be here.

The study of numerology can help you to understand not only yourself but also others with whom you come in contact. Numerology is one of the keys to unlock the potential within you as you attempt to achieve Socrates' maxim: "Man, know thyself." This study can give you a wealth of insight into your innate abilities and show you how to develop this potential.

In his book *Occult Medicine Can Save Your Life* (Bantam Books, 1977) Dr. C. Norman Shealy speaks of his experiences in diagnostic work as director of the famed Pain Rehabilitation Center in La Crosse, Wisconsin with professionals in the fields of numerology, astrology, palmistry, clairvoyance and other occult sciences. He states: "Now I feel the medical schools should offer courses in astrology and the other occult sciences, at least to familiarize the young doctors-to-be with these tools."

The two little books comprising this volume have been out of print for about 20 years. *The Secret in Your Name* is a basic beginning book which gives all the major rules of numerology and is especially valuable for the interpretation of the letters of the alphabet. A clear understanding of these interpretations will enhance your perception and enable you to apply this knowledge to many phases of your life.

The author, Helen Houston, was a lady of high-minded inspiration—beautiful inside and outside. I had the pleasure of attending one of her workshops, and her knowledge in her field was so vast that the little of her work which is left should open many avenues to the serious student. She was a lovely soul who graced the world with her presence.

The second book, *Your Number and Your Destiny*, truly belongs in the more advanced phases of numerology, but it can still be put to practical use. Almost every person who reads about his final number (called by some numerologists the Maturity Number) will say: "How could anyone know or understand so well these inner strivings which I hope to achieve?" It is the most extensive work ever written on this particular phase of numerology.

These two books should provide a good introduction to what numerology can do to help you in your pursuit of knowledge about yourself. There are now many other texts which go into the study more deeply, one of the newest and best being *Numerology: the Complete Guide* by Matthew Goodwin (Newcastle Publishing Co., Inc., 1981—2 vols., $25.90).

May the doors to wisdom and self-knowledge continue to open to all who read, study and apply the knowledge in these books and lead each of you along the path to true fulfillment.

Dorothy B. Hughes

Seattle, Washington
March 1982

BOOK ONE

THE SECRET IN YOUR NAME

HELEN HOUSTON

Author's Preface

The purpose of this book is to supply some much-needed information on a subject which has been receiving wide public recognition recently: Numerology, or the Science of Vibration of Numbers.

It is not my intention to go into tiresome details, furnish proofs or trace the history and origin of Numerology, but to bring out its practical side, capable of scientific application to the solution of daily problems, thus adding to the happiness and usefulness of your life.

By careful study of the following pages, you will find much that is helpful in your own life and in the lives of your friends and acquaintances. This knowledge can also be successfully applied in uncovering the character traits of strangers you meet in daily life, giving before-hand knowledge of the characteristics of each individual from the letters of his name. But the scope of its application does not end here. The Science of Vibration rightly understood and applied builds your character, expands your consciousness and broadens your vision and outlook on life. It can make you more tolerant of the faults and shortcomings of others by enabling you to understand more fully their problems and struggles in life. You will no longer condemn, but instead, try to help. This powerful knowledge places in your hands the most precious gift of all: the Key to Self Knowledge.

ONE

Introduction

The art of reading names and words through color vibration, sound vibration and numerical correspondence is very old in theory and practice. It dates back to ancient Greece, Egypt, Persia and other great nations of antiquity and permeates their esoteric teachings.

The Science of Numbers is based on the declaration: THERE IS NO CHANCE. ALL IS LAW AND MATHEMATICAL ORDER. GOD GEOMETRIZES.

Modern thought defines God as the Universal Principle of Life Infinite, finding expression in all things visible and invisible, and ruling the entire universe by the orderly working of Eternal Law, even to the most minute detail.

The nearest approach that can be made to evolve the "Inner Man," which is the "Image of the Creator," is through the knowledge and use of the Laws of Life contained in the Spirit of Mathematics. We are forced to deal with effects only; the Cause has ever been and ever will be represented as an "unknown quantity." The Cause—Cause of Life—God.

The universal law through which mankind deals with effects is the LAW OF MAGNETIC ATTRACTION. Every individual soul establishes for itself a Magnetic Center and becomes the image, so to speak, of the Original.

Under the Universal Law of Attraction, each person has attracted the name he or she bears, and could not have received any other. This law governs all things, even the naming of children, for as soon as a child is conceived, it sends forth radiations or vibrations of life and thus becomes a spiritual magnet, attracting to itself all that is needed for its development.

There is an electro-magnetic force working through and in everything. The mother attracts the child, and the innate nature of the child attracts to itself the name that corresponds to it. If parents understood this law, children would be better understood and developed along the lines of greatest possibilities.

Every child as an ego attracts its parents, or the path it comes through to earth life, by the Law of Attraction. "Like attracts like." Therefore, there was never a child born that did not partake in choosing its parents to a greater or lesser degree.

The influence of the environment upon the unborn reflects 90%. The mother as a formative principle in all nature, by the understanding of this law, creates the future of the child.

Life is the fundamental principle of our being. The cell or life germ is recognized as the beginning of manifested life. The character O in letters and zero or cipher (0) in figures represent this cell. Letters were derived from numbers, and numbers were taken from the cipher or this cell. The cell (0) is therefore the seed of the universe, the beginning of all things.

Spoken language is made up of words, and words are made up of letters representing sounds having color vibrations. Letters were originally borrowed from figures, which were used to represent creative force, or vibration, which is first motion, then light, followed by intelligence, knowledge and wisdom. This is just as capable of demonstration as a mathematical problem.

The main object in the analysis of character by means of the letters in the name is to recognize the innate possibilities in the mentality of each person, and thus assist him or her into fuller expression of the beautiful and perhaps unknown qualities that are lying dormant and can be brought out and put to use. Thought determines mental attitude, and mental attitude determines character.

TWO

The Key to Vibration

The Law of Vibration explains the rhythmical correspondence of numbers and letters. Vibration is the tremulous motion of the life wave manifested in all things. It is the law by which the human soul reaches from the physical sense to the spiritual consciousness that is infinite.

Numbers and letters call into action certain forces always present in the vibratory waves of the Universe, and these forces act and react upon the life and environment of the individual according to his relation to them as shown by the number vibration of the letters in the name and the date of birth.

The unfoldment of human consciousness is accomplished in cycles of emergence. Each cycle progresses and completes itself in an orderly sequence of nine degrees.

There are nine primary numbers: 1-2-3-4-5-6-7-8-9. All others are only combinations of these nine.

The letters of the alphabet have their numerical correspondence as follows:

1	—	A	J	S
2	—	B	K	T
3	—	C	L	U
4	—	D	M	V
5	—	E	N	W
6	—	F	O	X
7	—	G	P	Y
8	—	H	Q	Z
9	—	I	R	

To analyze a name, place the numbers corresponding to each of the letters under the name. Then add the numbers. Add the sum again, until you have one number for an answer. Repeat the same process with surname and middle name.

EXAMPLE:

HAROLD	WALTER	SMITH
819634	513259	14928

$$(31)\ 4\ +\ (25)\ 7\ +\ (24)\ 6\ =\ 17\ =\ 8$$

We find that the vibration of Harold is 4, of Walter 7, and of Smith 6.

THE DESTINY NUMBER

To obtain the Destiny Number of the name, it is necessary to add together the vibrations of each separate name.

Thus:

The vibration of Harold is 4
The vibration of Walter is 7
The vibration of Smith is......... 6

Total   17 = 1 + 7 = 8 Destiny
                                    Number

The Destiny Number is of great importance. It is the number through which one gains experience in life. It represents the first definite vibration that affects the individual, sometimes called the Number of Fate.

THE SPIRITUAL URGE NUMBER

To find the Spiritual Urge Number, add the vowels of the first name, middle name and surname, reducing the numbers until a single number is obtained for an answer.

EXAMPLE:

7	+	6	+	9	= 22* or
___		___		__	Spiritual Urge Number
1 6		1 5		9	

HAROLD + WALTER + SMITH

The Spiritual Urge Number shows the degree of inherent ability, accumulated knowledge and wisdom brought from former lives, in order to meet the requirements of daily life. In all names the vowels stand for the innate spiritual nature, and the consonants for the physical expression. Together they tell the true story of the character of the individual. The first vowel in the name is the center, or key-note, to the character and is the master, just as the key-note in music is the master of the whole melody.

While the first vowel gives the key-note to the character, it is greatly modified by the consonants that follow or precede, and by the other vowels that follow.

THE PHYSICAL LIFE NUMBER

The Physical Life Number is derived from the consonants of the full name.

---

*Numbers 22 and 11 are Master Vibrations and are never reduced to a single number.

HAROLD	WALTER	SMITH
8 9 34	5 32 9	14 28

(24) 6 + (19) 1 + (15) 6 = 13 = 1 + 3 = 4

or Physical Life Number

The Physical Life Number shows the manner in which you impress other people. It is your outer personality.

THE VOCATION NUMBER

To obtain the Vocation Number, add together the day, month,* and year of birth.

EXAMPLE:

$$\text{June} \quad 17, \quad 1895$$
$$6 \qquad 8 \qquad \underline{23}$$
$$6 + 8 + 5 \ = 19$$

$$1 + 9 = 10 = 1 \text{ or Vocation Number}$$

The Vocation Number shows the lesson one has come to learn in this life. It has a decided influence and is next in importance to the Destiny Number. It shows the real purpose in life. One's life work should be planned according to the demands of this number.

*Months are rated according to their places in the calendar. Thus January is 1, February is 2, March is 3, December is 12, etc.

THREE

The Significance of Letters

Vibration is life, and life is numbers in vibration. Every number, letter, geometrical form, musical scale and tone is a center of creative energy.

Letters are symbols of vibration in the inner soul world, and every letter is a medium or channel through which subtle forces act upon the individual.

Names are composed of letters and have forms. Their messages of good or evil are constantly conveyed to the nerves and atoms of the human body, also leaving their impression upon the surroundings. The laws governing name vibrations are as accurate as an electric instrument, producing formations and results.

The name number has a certain value in helping us to see what tasks lie before us in this life, while the first name given at birth, called the "Book of Life," or register, remains the same in its significance. We must work out its vibration, which is the result of previous lives. A new name properly chosen will help to make the conditions easier and will harmonize discordant elements in our character. No one should change his or her name haphazardly without first understanding the meaning of each letter and to what extent such change would help to work out the lessons in this life shown by the Vocation Number.

The Vocation Number shows the lesson you came to learn in this life, while your name indicates the manner in which you are working it out. The name is the *active* vibration and creates in your life the qualities it stands for.

The name is composed of letters, each having its particular significance. Some letters give expression, others stand for poise, perseverance, order or leadership, while others give inspiration, creative ability, courage, etc. It is the combination of the different attributes that makes the name either strong or weak in its vibration. The first letter of the name and the first vowel wield great influence over the rest of the letters and tell us much about the individual.

THE LETTER A

A is the greatest and noblest of all letters and stands for ambition, aspiration and purity. It endows its possessor with a restless and pioneering nature, not content to stay long in one place but seeking change and adventure. A gives energy, much self-reliance and independence in thought and action. Those coming under the influence of this vibration are the beginners and not the finishers. A's will not take advice from others, but must learn through experience. Do things in an original way. Natural leaders. Must learn to overcome the self. A's cause activity in other letters of the name. Too many A's cause the individual to be too impulsive. When out of harmony, A is very selfish, egotistic and stubborn.

THE LETTER B

B denotes ability to construct, whether on the material or spiritual plane. Resourceful and inventive. B in the beginning of a name denotes order. B people like to stay in one place. Very intuitive, dreamers, mediators and diplomats. Great mother love. Extremely sensitive and often timid, lacking self-assertiveness. Need encouragement and appreciation. People born on the 2nd and 20th of any month should not begin the first name with the letter B. Lovers of home, need companionship. Cannot work alone. Usually have very pleasing personality, gentle, quiet, lovable disposition and fine temperament. B stands for co-operation, tact and diplomacy. Duality, negative and positive. Greatest fault is self-depreciation. Need to cultivate strong will.

THE LETTER C

C stands for the outward expression of the Christ Principle. Very creative mentality. Vivid imagination; often exaggerate unknowingly. Find happiness in making others happy. Sociable and easy to get along with. C stands for utmost in self-expression. Music, art, acting, singing, dancing, and painting are some of the occupations of C people. Should guard the throat. If out of harmony, tend to scattered forces, and have difficulty in accumulating money. Must overcome indecision. Sometimes overrate their strength. C's see over large spaces mentally.

THE LETTER D

D stands for practical discrimination, straightforwardness and justice. Marked intellectual tendencies, keen and discerning mind. Sometimes over-critical. Have a tendency to oppose everything, therefore stand in their own light. Interested in scientific studies and seek proofs and facts rather than theories. D's love home life. Tenacious in love affairs. The letter D represents the square, therefore enclosed and shut in. Love appreciation and a pat on the back. Need urging. Have difficulty in expressing themselves. Like to be alone at times. People vibrating to D are honest, true and constant, and will fight for justice. Hard workers and like to save money. Good judges of values. D gives temper, which should be controlled, otherwise it will affect health and spoil opportunities for success. Should live close to nature. Belong to the business world, manufacturing, mining, real estate, etc. Order and intensity of purpose are marked characteristics of this vibration.

THE LETTER E

The vibration of this letter brings changes, travel and adventure to its owner. E's like to delve deeply into the mysteries of life. Interested in spiritual matters. Have foresight, versatility of mind and ability to learn with ease anything they are interested in, especially pertaining to words, writing, foreign languages, etc. Strong in personal opinions, energetic, enthusiastic and good talkers. Believe in strict justice. Very adaptable and have executive ability. Nervous temperament, yet carry an appearance of coolness. Like research work. With many E's in a name one will have a tendency to be too impulsive and changeable. E's need O's to slow them down.

THE LETTER F

F stands for Cosmic Love, Christ Force in nature, guardianship. A very constructive vibration. Have intuition and a deep insight into the hidden truths. Absorb knowledge, but never learn by rule. Cheerfulness is the key-note of F vibration. Like quiet and peace. Do not like criticism and cannot take advice. Firm in opinions, whether right or wrong. Not easily convinced. Usually successful in business. Never worry much. Reliable, honest and conscientious; hold truth to be the greatest of all virtues. F's have great love of harmony and are fond of art and beauty. Need home and companionship in order to be happy. Lucky and like to speculate.

THE LETTER G

G stands for determination. Those coming under the influence of this vibration are very original in thought and action and are inclined toward intellectual and philosophical pursuits. Lack of self-expression is one great disadvantage of this vibration, therefore they are often musunderstood by others. People having many G's have much patience and the ability to assimilate knowledge, often developing a great store of wisdom. G's should never go into partnership in business. Should live on all three planes (physical, mental and spiritual) for harmony. The undeveloped side of G stands for struggle, opposition and misfortune. G's often possess psychic powers. Imagination is a notable attribute of this vibration, and detemination to overcome obstacles is another.

THE LETTER H

H is the power to draw. Capable of great achievement in business and finance. Have executive ability and should be leaders and have charge over many people. Usually fluent talkers and good mixers. Very active. Analytical and seek proofs of spiritual things. Depend more on reason than in-tuition. Fond of travel and outdoor sports. Have literary abilities and make interesting letter writers. H's out of har-mony with birth have many ups and downs in life. Difficult to reform or change. Very unselfish and loyal.

THE LETTER I

I stands for the I Am consciousness. Dreamers. Usually over-sensitive; their feelings are easily hurt. A very personal vibra-tion. People carrying I's in the name are very intuitive and sympathetic. Make inspirational speakers, lecturers, mis-sionaries, actors and musicians. I's have a tendency to reflect the environment and should have periods of medita-tion. Very intense in whatever they do. Go to extremes. Marked intellectual tendencies. Analytical and critical, forceful and dictatorial, quick to see faults before virtues. I's have deep love of home but are often unhappy in this respect. Have stromg imagination and sometimes are too serious and inclined to see the pathetic side of life. Out of harmony, have troubles, sacrifices and sufferings; of all vibrations are the most unhappy. Very strong in personal opinions, cannot be convinced otherwise. Should live close to nature.

THE LETTER J

J stands for leadership. Strong imagination, originality of thought and action. Have inventive ability. J's are interested in religious matters. Idealistic, always work for improvement. Most are moral and clean-minded. People coming under this vibration are very systematic and orderly and have clearness of mental vision. J's suffer through affection. Faith is killed when friendship is broken. Generally good natured and of happy disposition. Greatly influenced by environment and should make decisions when alone. J holds latent powers subject to development when rightly understood. Money-making is very gratifying. Very unhappy without it.

THE LETTER K

K carries a very high spiritual vibration. Very broad and tolerant. Dreamers. Difficult to understand. Strong in likes and dislikes. Extremists. Should keep to the straight and narrow path for success and health. K's are intuitive and possess spiritual power. They are very old souls and have the wisdom of the ages stored in their subconscious minds. Their mission is to teach, lead and aid others. They must sacrifice their own immediate good for the good of many or their greatest success is not reached. They should prepare themselves for teaching, or for giving spiritual light. People of this vibration are refined and appreciative of the beautiful and artistic. Do not like to have many people for close friends. K should never shirk duty. Should strive to develop the spiritual nature. Out of harmony, often have tragedies in life.

THE LETTER L

L stands for love of justice. Energetic and full of push, always searching for new things. People of this vibration find happiness in service. Make good managers and organizers.

Want credit and public approval. Inclined to worry un-
necessarily. Usually have a good voice and sweetness of
manner. People born on the 12th of any month should
never begin name with L. When out of harmony, are likely
to have throat trouble.

THE LETTER M

M stands for regeneration and reconstruction on all planes.
Should rule and lead. Capable. Have executive ability. M is
a highly spiritual vibration; beneficent and sympathetic,
alive with the spirit of life. Fond of travel, expecially by
water. Often very alone and difficult to get acquainted with.
Should always follow their own intuition and not be led
by others. M's are natural homemakers. Capable along
mechanical lines. Intellectual.

THE LETTER N

If N is the first letter of your name you are careful with
details. Considered a successful letter. Indicates brilliant
mentality, adaptability and versatility. N rules the body.
Often nervous and restless people. Like to change and
travel. Should never talk of private business affairs. Out of
harmony, affects the health. N's are inclined to marry
young, or very late in life. Make interesting speakers and
lawyers. Analytical. Will fight for justice.

THE LETTER O

O stands for concentration. Those coming under this vibration are usually lucky and always protected and taken care
of. O's draw things to themselves—knowledge, friends,
money, gifts, etc. Have pleasing personality. Faithful and
true. Inclined to use own judgment. Change home often for
something better. Do not like to work with hands for a living. Suffer in silence. Too many O's make one too slow to
make up his mind. Needs A's to quicken him. Stubborn.

THE LETTER P

If P is the first letter of your name, you are liberally endowed with spiritual powers. Intuition and prophetic vision are your inborn attributes. P denotes wonderful character. Very capable. Interested in transcendental science and philosophy. P's learn through intuition and not from books. Have an uncanny psychic power which enables them to understand things unseen. Difficult to get acquainted with. Like to be alone and meditate. Very lonely. Have great will power and moral courage.

THE LETTER Q

Q stands for hope and cheerfulness. Excellent letter for business, can deal with large corporations. Executive ability. Assume responsibility. Good providers and free with money. Proud spirited, just and square. Like to take long journeys, generally across the sea. Seldom happy in marriage; either marry too often or not at all. With harmonious name, can rise to eminence and distinguished success. Q's cater to people of distinction.

THE LETTER R

R stands for keen discrimination. R's belong to the intellectual world. Writers, teachers, artists, poets, etc. Natural leaders. Liable to extremes. Generally bear a cross. Usually have old people to take care of. R's are fond of abstract learning and find pleasure in balancing and comparing things. Have the gift of inspiring confidence in other people without effort. They are keen thinkers and have an inborn ability to store up knowledge. More than one R in a name has a tendency to over-action and nervous exhaustion, therefore, should guard health. R's should learn application and persistence. R causes delays.

THE LETTER S

S stands for regeneration. People coming under this vibration are born mystics and of religious turn of mind, but will not accept orthodox creeds or ceremony. Original in thought and action. Independent thinkers. S follows the spiritual path. Very alone, often hard to please. Out of harmony, S is considered an unfortunate letter and causes accidents; feet and ears liable to be afflicted. Should live near the water.

THE LETTER T

This vibration is much like that of the letter B. T has natural mother instinct. Capable in domestic arts. Very intuitive and somewhat exacting, yet very devoted to its own. Gentle and calm disposition, interested in spiritual matters. Natural peacemaker. T often indicates a change of home. Love to have things their own way. Out of harmony, tendency to headaches and brain fever.

THE LETTER U

U stands for self-protection. People coming under this vibration are subject to emotional disturbances. Will rise out of any state of depression; will not stay down. Have dignity and exclusiveness. Warm-hearted, faithful, good parents and natural protectors of the helpless. Do not like advice. Will listen and then do as they please. Fond of travel. Have passion for study. Like poetry, literature and abstract sciences. Analytical and careful of detail. U's out of harmony scatter forces; undertake many things, seldom finish any. Often destroy own happiness by impatience. Should study music and voice. Conservation should be their motto.

THE LETTER V

V stands for strong individuality. People coming under this vibration belong to the business world. Very capable, hopeful, steadfast and loyal. Strong in likes and dislikes. Generous with money to the point of extravagance. Cannot say "no." Usually successful in business, especially in ships and shipping, importing and exporting. Fond of travel by water. Cannot succeed in home town. Must push out into the world to become successful and independent. Should have interest outside of home. Depression their worst enemy. Need praise and appreciation.

THE LETTER W

The possessors of this vibration are proud-spirited, versatile and clever in speech and writing. Learn easily. Prosperous in business. Believe strongly in law and order. Fond of plants and flowers. Successful architects and mechanical engineers. Like to study plants for their curative properties. Make good diagnosticians and nature doctors when they lead their ambition in that direction. These people are wonderful with their cultivated talents. Have strong love of nature and have to love someone to live.

THE LETTER X

Success in worldly matters is the keynote of this vibration. X people are artistic and very talented, usually make good actors. Great dressers. Like to associate with people in high or influential positions. Like to lead and rule, but are very considerate. Should have business interests and many friends. Do not worry much. Like peace and quiet. Danger of falls. Should beware of high places.

THE LETTER Y

Y stands for intuition. Those coming under this vibration are endowed with psychic power and often have prophetic dreams. Have inborn talents for penetrating mysteries and can uncover the truths of hidden things. Belong to the professional world; make good lawyers. Very dependable.

Greatest fault lies in underestimating their ability. Should obey and follow their first impressions. When out of harmony, live on inflamed emotions. Often feel they never receive all they give. Should follow the normal plane of life for health and prosperity.

THE LETTER Z

Z stands for extremists. Those bearing this vibration have much self-confidence, push and energy. A wonderful financial letter when associated with big things. Possess executive ability. Can organize and promote. Z's cater to people of distinction. Proud-spirited. Inclined to magnify and exaggerate. Should guard against excesses. Often big eaters. Z's have the power and ability to control others. A good letter for diplomatic and secret service work.

FOUR

The Vibration Of Numbers

There are nine primary numbers upon which the Science of Vibration is built. The cipher or zero (0) is not considered a number, for it does not represent any definite quantity unless associated with other numbers. It has no interpretation that can be considered tangible, therefore is beyond the sphere of human existence. Its form, the circle, is symbolic of the Infinite, without beginning or ending.

All numbers above 9 are composite numbers and partake of the meaning of the primary numbers of which they are composed. The number 15 is composed of 1 and 5 and reduces to the primary number 6. Nevertheless, the predominant characteristic of number 15 would be that of number 6, modified by the characteristics of numbers 1 and 5. Similarly, the same method of analysis is applied to any composite number. The numbers of the name, destiny, vocation, spiritual urge, physical life and those of day of birth are analyzed in like manner. The important part in analyzing the vibrations of numbers is to have a thorough understanding of the primary numbers 1-2-3-4-5-6-7-8-9.

THE NUMBER 1

Number 1 is the father of all numbers. It is the symbol of unity. It stands for ambition, originality, independence and firmess of purpose. Number 1 is a natural leader. Very original in thought and action, therefore very creative. Explorers, pioneers, promoters and organizers. 1 has a very forceful nature, very determined and active, therefore aggressive. 1 is the number of concentration, centralization, application and effort, with great desire for achievement. 1 makes other numbers active. 1's can think for themselves. Will not take advice and often become stubborn. 1's are the beginners and not the finishers. Self-centered and should guard against selfishness. 1's do things in an original way. Exact about details. Inventive by nature. Very determined and overcome obstacles by meeting issues squarely. Believe in their own ability. Have dignity.

On the undeveloped plane 1's are dictatorial, selfish, egotistic, arrogant and unkind to others, cunning and cynical.

THE NUMBER 2

Number 2 stands for duality, balance and equilibrium. Positive and negative. Collectors and builders.

Those having the 2 vibration are diplomatic, tactful, social, considerate and kind. Cooperation is an outstanding characteristic of number 2; therefore can go into partnership. Cannot stand alone. Like to stay in one place. 2's are gentle and quiet. Love home, peace and harmony. Have good judgment and foresight. Make good diplomats, arbitrators, teachers, nurses, writers, lawyers, etc. Have patience and continuity of thought. Greatest fault of this number is self-depreciation. Often timid and sensitive, and easily discouraged. Should cultivate will power and aggressiveness.

THE NUMBER 3

Number 3 stands for expression. Creative, especially along aritstic lines. Very independent, both in speech and manners. 3's have ability to adapt themselves to circumstances. Very enthusiastic and happy. Find joy in service. Versatility is one great characteristic of number 3 people. Make good actors, singers, poets, lecturers and prophets. Should have education along many lines. Natural leaders. Intellectual. Very energetic. Scattered forces, indecision and self-pity are their great faults. Should learn conservation. Subject to throat trouble, therefore should not have L's in the name.

THE NUMBER 4

Number 4 stands for justice, discrimination and success. Number 4 works on the intellectual plane. Keen and discerning. Practical, steadfast and reliable. Capable along mechanical lines. Have strength of purpose and will power. Hard workers, industrious, painstaking and thorough. They build for the future. Find their happiness in a field of regular endeavor. Do not like to change. 4 is a physical number, therefore they do not always depend on intuition, but on reason and intellect. Interested in efficiency. Are methodical, systematic, orderly, analytical, honest, masters of detail and routine. Have much patience. Economical and like to save money. Ambitions are of a personal nature. Most conscientious and faithful. Can depend on them when they give their word. 4's are lovers of home. Should have broad education along practical and scientific lines. 4's usually have to work for their money. Cannot gamble. Endurance is a noted characteristic of this vibration.

THE NUMBER 5

Number 5 stands for changes, enterprises and mental activity. Versatility and enthusiasm are noted characteristics of this number. Have an inborn desire for travel and adventure. Interested in new things. Fearless and indifferent to danger. Can make friends easily, good mixers, very active and energetic, quick and brilliant mentally, interested in anything that will afford a new experience. Have stong investigating instinct, good judges of human nature. Make good salesmen, lecturers, newspaper reporters, detectives, theatrical managers, transportation, or any work requiring movement, emergency powers and variety. Their lives are filled with events, often of short duration. 5's are the speculators and gamblers. Very unstable temperament. People of this vibration cannot be properly labeled. Have the ability to learn easily anything upon which their interest is centered.

THE NUMBER 6

Number 6 is the number of harmony, cheerfulness and hope. It is an even number and indicates a well balanced nature. Considered very fortunate. 6's have a tolerant disposition, kind and good-hearted. Very reliable and most dependable. They are naturally unselfish and peaceful by nature, but they will never fail to fight for principles in which they believe. 6 is a cosmic mother, sympathetic; therefore 6's make good nurses, doctors, teachers community workers, institution managers, dieticians, business managers, welfare workers, etc. They are home lovers and cling closely to their families. 6 is an absorbent number, therefore 6's gather knowledge. Never learn by rule. Always well able to take care of themselves. Proud-spirited. Hard to convince.

THE NUMBER 7

Seven is a mystic number. Stands for intuition, silent wisdom, perfection, spirituality and culture. People of this vibration are always a mystery to others, and are seldom understood and appreciated. They have the ability to assimilate knowledge and often develop a great store of wisdom, but seldom give it out. Have much self-confidence, poise and a firm will. They are intuitive, psychic and highly imaginative. Often possess strange and uncanny mental powers. Like to be alone and undisturbed, although at other times they can be affable and even talkative. 7's possess strong intellectual qualities, are far-seeing and philosophical. Have much patience. Should have a broad education in fine arts. The vocations of this number are the ministry, psychology, writing, medicine, law, real estate, etc. 7's are not inclined to go into partnerships. Should work in an individual capacity where they are the absolute authority in their own realm. Loneliness is often the lot of this vibration. Lack of self-expression is a great disadvantage to number 7. Should cultivate an interest in the active affairs of life; bring to the surface the hidden power and seek to apply knowledge in a practical way.

THE NUMBER 8

Eight is the number of material success. People of this vibration have great capabilities as executives and should be in positions where they have charge over others. Can assume responsibility. Have good judgment in business matters. Leaders. Number 8 has literary ability. Good talkers. Make good lawyers and bankers. 8's like to stand well. Optimistic, full of push and energy. Out of harmony with birth, have many ups and downs in life. Analytical and critical and are always seeking for proofs of spiritual things. They do well in the fields of investment and speculation. They are born money-makers and find their supreme happiness in the use of this money-making power for the good of humanity. Their mission is to assist others to higher levels of freedom. To become really great they must guard against selfishness.

THE NUMBER 9

Number 9 is the last of the primary numbers and is the symbol of universal influence. It stands for the accumulation of all things and represents a high state of mental and spiritual development. 9's are the people with broad views, humanitarians and benefactors of humanity. Number 9 is typified by universal love. Must lead. Very intellectual, artistic and talented. People of this vibration are affable, humane, sympathetic and have the gift of winning affection. 9's have lots of imagination and intuition. Dreamers. Integrity is a noted characteristic of number 9. Very inspirational. Make good writers, artists, healers, humanitarian workers, lecturers, musicians, actors, landscape gardeners, ministers, teachers, metaphysicians and travelers. Out of harmony and on the undeveloped plane, 9's are selfish, miserly, destructive and sarcastic. Very unhappy.

THE NUMBER 11

Although number 11 is not a primary number, nevertheless it has a special significance, and is never reduced to 2 when it appears as a final number of name, birthdate, vocation, destiny, spiritual urge and physical life numbers. It is considered a Master Number. It stands for inspiration, wisdom and power. People vibrating to this number are very old souls in new bodies, having been through all the lessons of the preceding numbers. Their mission is to lead and aid others into better and larger ways. They are the priests of humanity, and should be the dispensers of spiritual knowledge. They are very alone and usually misunderstood by others. Often inventors and originators. They must sacrifice their immediate good for the good of many, or their greatest success is not reached. 11's often have tragedies in life.

THE NUMBER 22

Number 22 is also considered a Master Number, just like number 11, but its influence is of a different character. 22 stands for mastery of the physical. Through obedience to higher laws and intelligent cooperation the possessor of this vibration can become a master of himself and of his environment. 22 is most successful in occupations of a professional nature, such as statesmanship, diplomatic work, advisory work in law, philanthropy, humanitarian fields, etc. 22 is usually successful in money matters but often becomes extravagant. They tend to be extremists, and should guard against excesses. 22's have delicate bodies. Should strive to build health. Must have a name in harmony to be a success.

FIVE

The Three Cycles Of Life

Broadly speaking, your life is divided into three periods, or cycles, which are governed by the digits of your birth path. During each period certain lessons are to be learned, which are indicated by the number governing it. You should therefore engage in the activities and cultivate the qualities which vibration indicates.

The digit of your month of birth governs the first 27 years of life.

The digit of your day or birth governs the second 27 years of life (from 27 through 54).

The third cycle or period begins from your 54th year and controls the balance of life. It is governed by the digit of your year of birth.

This completes the trinity of 1-2-3. 1 which corresponds to the month, is spirit entering matter, so we are moulding the clay, or body and mind, in the first 27 years, preparing for the next period of 2, which is collecting the material for the next period of 3, or complete expression.

The combined vibrations of the digits of the month, day and year of birth give the Vocation Number, the influence of which is of great importance during the entire life. The sooner you learn the lessons of the digits of month and day, the sooner you will pass into the vibration of the digit of the year, completing the third cycle, and thus arriving at your ultimate goal.

LIFE'S CHALLENGE

Every individual has a Challenge in life. Through Numbers one can determine what this challenge is and can begin building into his character the attributes and qualities needed for rounded development. Challenge denotes that particular handicap or weakness of character which he must overcome by strengthening or cultivating the good and desirable traits and qualities in its place.

To find the Challenge Number of an individual born June 18, 1902, observe the following rules:

Reduce the month, day and year to final digits. Thus: The number of June is 6. Birthday is 18, 1 + 8 = 9. Year is 1902, 1 + 9 + 0 + 2 = 12, 1 + 2 = 3. The digits are 6, 9, 3. Next, subtract the digit of the month (6) from the digit of birthday (9); 9 – 6 = 3, or first remainder. The next step is to subtract the digit of the year (3) from the digit of the birthday (9); 9 – 3 = 6, or second remainder. The last step is to subtract the smaller remainder from the larger. Thus 6 – 3 = 3, or Challenge Number.

Note: Should the digit of the birthday be smaller than the digits of month and year, simply reverse the process of subtraction.

To illustrate:

Born August 3, 1906
    8   3   (16)7

By subtracting 3 from 8, the first remainder is 5.

By subtracting 3 from 7, the second remainder is 4.

By subtracting the smaller remainder from the larger, 5 – 4 = 1, or Challenge Number.

Should both remainders be the same, the challenge would be zero (0).

THE SIGNIFICANCE OF
CHALLENGE NUMBERS

1 – The 1 is a challenge against your individuality. Must act according to your own opinion.

2 – The challenge is sensitiveness.

3 – The challenge is against your expression.

4 – You will have to do things yourself, gain by your own endeavors.

5 – Challenge is against your freedom.

6 – Challenge is against your ideals, against your love for humanity.

7 – Challenge is against your generosity. Through great understanding you will win.

8 – Challenge. 8's know they have great power latent in their lives to meet their challenge.

9 – Not found.

If zero is your challenge you are always capable of meeting and overcoming your obstacles.

THE VIBRATION OF CITIES

Cities have their characters and destinies just like individuals. The name of the city indicates the quality of vibration, the kind of people it attracts and the manner of its growth and development. Just as countries differ in topography and climate, so do they differ in vibration, and different cities and different parts of the same city attract residents of similar tastes.

To analyze the name of a city, find its Destiny Number by adding together all the letters of its name. The vowels or the spiritual urge of a city show the quality of subjective or spiritual vibration. Cities attract their people through the vowels.

Individuals having the same vowels in their names as those of the city, will feel at home and can attain success and happiness much sooner there. When the vowels and Destiny Number of the individual are the same as those of the city, he will do extremely well there.

EXAMPLE:

$$N\ E\ W \qquad Y\ O\ R\ K$$
$$\underline{5\ 5\ 5} \qquad \underline{7\ 6\ 9\ 2}$$
$$(15)\ 6 + (24)\ 6\ = 12 = 1 + 2 = 3$$
$$\text{or Destiny Number}$$

The vowels are E, or 5, and O, or 6. Total 11.

This city well shows the broad surface the vibration 3 expresses. It should be a happy meeting place for all kinds of people. Its vowels, E and O, call for men and women who are vibrating to the highest human vibration, that of the 11.

The vibration of any city, state, or country can be found by the same process.

BOOK TWO

YOUR NUMBER
AND YOUR DESTINY

JUNO JORDAN

(JUNO KAYY WALTON)

Much credit is due to the beloved teachers and students of the California Institute of Numerical Research, Inc., for the material of this book. Years were spent gathering statistics which prove its precepts. The blessings of these teachers is given to all who find themselves through its instruction.

ONE

Your Number And Your Destiny

YOUR NAME

Why were your parents so anxious to select a suitable name for you at the time of your birth? Because your name signifies your destiny and is the medium through which your character is expressed. It is the signboard or blueprint along your road to success. Your parents sensed this and unconsciously named you for the particular character you were destined by birth to express.

Your name carries a message to you, for names are symbols of vibratory force and thought. The message of your name and the purpose which it represents are registered in the ethers of sound and force and re-echo down the pathway of your life to challenge you with its requirements and opportunities. It calls out from the four quarters of the world the people, experiences and conditions to which you are attuned, and links you—whether you will or not—with that which you must do or be. It brings you face to face with your own at every turn of life's pathway.

YOUR NUMBER

There is a number accompanying your name, for hidden in your full name and age is your REALITY NUMBER, and the finding of this number is of vital importance to you.

3

If you are uncertain about your future or your place in life, this means you do not know your number and are missing many opportunities because you do not recognize your "call" or "cue" when it is given to you by your number.

When you find this number you gain the key which unlocks the mysteries of your being and points the way to your greatest success.

Until you are about thirty-five or forty years of age, the promise of your REALITY NUMBER and its privileges may not be fully realized. Or you may feel that the requirements of your number are a handicap rather than an opportunity, and that it is impossible for you to become what it suggests. You may even be older before you truly sense this is the pathway of true development.

This is because the success which it offers must be lived up to and earned, for your REALITY NUMBER represents the goal of your life—typifies the essence of all your experiences—and is what you will become when you have reached the peak of attainment. It is what you can and should develop or cultivate for the richness and fullness of success to the end of your days.

The REALITY is not an active characteristic early in life, but the talents and abilities of the REAL SELF may be strongly sensed at an early age. This is the best time to grasp the idea and to plan for its future development, even in the face of obstacles, for after all, problems and difficulties help to bring out a finer power and stronger character. The duality between the struggle and the opportunity—the handicap and the reward—is the true law of growth.

Often during the first part of life there are so many obstacles in the way that many people give up or are too uncertain to make the real effort and eventually become "just ordinary" people, finding their latter days of life dependent and of no real value, when they might have become great or found a place of real usefulness had they followed the dimly sensed REALITY urge. But it is never too late to mend one's ways, and if the effort is made to be what the REALITY proclaims, the experience leads to a new birth and realization—for the inner nature or soul grasps at any opportunity to be itself. Self-knowledge then becomes an avenue to finer self-expression.

Many of the most important experiences of the lifetime come through the REALITY influence. At some time everyone has the experience of meeting its demands through a feeling of unrest and discontent. This gives a desire to do something big, and if the goal of the REALITY indication is not understood, mistakes follow this unrest. But if the call of the number is answered and this signboard of destiny is followed, a forward step will be taken and a deep inner satisfaction will follow.

Everyone, consciously or unconsciously, expresses some degree of the latent quality of the REALITY NUMBER. Even though not fully developed, it influences the way one does things; colors the individual characteristics and tendencies, for the force behind the REALITY NUMBER stands for more than talent and opportunity. It is the symbol of the Ego, the archetype of the Divine Soul within each individual, and is the spiritual consciousness which many lives and rebirths have built into form.

* * * *

Sometimes the demand of the REALITY is not the desire of the individual, and other ambitions fill the mind. These should be combined with the activity of the REAL SELF, or the REALITY NUMBER, for when this is done many of the barriers and obstacles which stood in the way of the ambition fall away, leaving one free to rise in life until all desires are realized. Remember! Your REALITY NUMBER indicates your highest development after all other experiments have been lived through.

* * * *

Your REALITY NUMBER is found from the sum of your name and birth. Every letter of your name has a number, and the month, day and year of your birth also adds up to a number.

The following chart is the basis of figuring:

$$1\ 2\ 3\ 4\ 5\ 6\ 7\ 8\ 9$$

A B C D E F G H I
J K L M N O P Q R
S T U V W X Y Z

The numbers above the letters represent the numerical value of the letters in all names.

RULES

FIRST: Find your NAME NUMBER by placing the numbers above the letters in the chart under the same letters in your name. Add up each name and reduce to a single digit. Then add the digit or total of each name together and again reduce to a single digit. This final number will be your NAME NUMBER, and represents your field of activity, environment, association, expression, where you will do your work, the kind of people you will meet and what you will have to do for them. It is sometimes called the Destiny Number.

SECOND: Find your BIRTH NUMBER according to the numerical value of the calendar. Place under your month, day and year of birth the corresponding numbers, reducing all combinations of numbers to one number or single digit by adding. Give each month its calendar number, reducing to a single digit if the 10th, 11th or 12th months. If born after the ninth day of any month, reduce this date to a single digit by adding the two numbers together. Sum up the year in the same way and reduce to a single digit. Now add all three numbers together. This is your BIRTH NUMBER and represents the foundation upon which you stand, your talents, natural abilities and capabilities. It is what you draw upon for background for endeavor and the effort you must give to all your undertakings.

THIRD: Find your REALITY NUMBER—the most important number of all—by adding your NAME NUMBER and your

BIRTH NUMBER together. This is the total of all your power and represents your highest development—your real goal in life. It is your REAL SELF, for there is nothing more to build upon. It sums up every degree of vibration in your name and birth. It is the fruit of your labors.

EXAMPLE:

Note: The following name is given as an example, for his REALITY NUMBER appeared during the most important period of his life.

FIRST RULE:

```
F R A N K L I N    D E L A N O    R O O S E V E L T
6 9 1 5 2 3 9 5    4 5 3 1 5 6    9 6 6 1 5 4 5 3 2
  (40) 4      +    (24) 6    +      (41) 5    = 15 = 1 + 5 = 6 or
                                               NAME NUMBER
```

Reduce every combination of numbers to a single digit by adding the combinations. This is the rule in every case. Always use the *full name at birth,* regardless of present names or changes of location or spelling. It is the BIRTH NAME that gives the NAME NUMBER. Figure your own name according to the above example.

SECOND RULE:

> January 30, 1882
>
> 1   + 3 +(19) (10) 1 = 5 BIRTH NUMBER

January is the first month or 1; reduce 30 to 3 by adding the 3 and the 0. Add 1882; this equals 19. Complete this addition by adding 1 and 9, which gives 10; reduce to 1. Add 1 of month to 3 of birthday and 1 of year. This equals 5, which is the BIRTH NUMBER.

THIRD RULE:

> Add: NAME NUMBER   6
> BIRTH NUMBER   5
>
> (11) or 2 REALITY NUMBER

This number (11) 2 represents his ultimate goal, his REAL SELF and highest possibility in life. Your own REALITY NUMBER reveals the same thing; from birth to the end of life it is the signal in which direction you should turn for your greatest joy, work, service and ultimate attainment.

Interesting attractions between yourself and others will be shown later by further figuring, but for the present it is important for you to carefully consider your REAL SELF and your true possibilities through your REALITY NUMBER.

TWO

Reality Attractions

The charateristics of your REALITY NUMBER are developed through the daily experiences with the people who form your friendly associations and family life. Some of your deepest experiences come through those people who have in their names your own REALITY NUMBER. An instant attraction or strange antipathy may be felt according to this number, for someone who has your particular number may be strangely drawn to you for a mutual friendship, or in a similar way, a very unhappy experience, depending upon the position of the REALITY NUMBER in the other person's name.

POSITIONS

There are six important positions in a name where the REALITY NUMBER may appear, both in your own name and in the names of others. These must be taken into consideration when studying the REALITY attractions, for it is the position of the number rather than the number itself which reveals the possible harmony or disharmony.

You have figured three of these positions, and it is now necessary that further figuring be done to gain the remaining three positions and complete the chart of reference. The first three positions are again figured in the following chart, for illustration:

NOTE: Always use the full name at birth and the month, day and year of birth as it was given in the native land or country. The original name, regardless of changes of country or spelling, is the one to be used for the correct REALITY NUMBER.

1st Position — HEART NUMBER
    (sum of the letters a–e–i–o–u)

2nd Position — PERSONALITY NUMBER
    (sum of the consonants only)

3rd Position — NAME (DESTINY) NUMBER
    (sum of all the letters in the name)

4th Position — BIRTH (ABILITY) NUMBER
    (sum of the month, day and year of birth)

5th Position — REALITY NUMBER
    (sum of the name number and birth number)

6th Position — PERSONAL YEAR NUMBER
    (sum of your month and day of birth only
    added to the current year)

CHART FOR FIGURING

Position

1st: (10) 1   +   (12) 3   +   (22) 4   = 8 HEART
      1   9   5 1 6   66 5 5   NUMBER
                                         (vowels)

   FRANKLIN   DELANO   ROOS'EVELT

2nd: 69 523 5   4 3 5   9 1 4 32
     (30) 3   +   (12) 3   +   (19) 1   = 7 PERSONALITY
                                      NUMBER
                                      (consonants)

3rd: <u>69152395   453156   966154532</u>
       (40) 4   +   (24) 6   +   (41) 5   = 15 = 1 + 5 =
                                            6 DESTINY or
                                            NAME NUMBER
                                            (all numbers)

4th: January 30,   <u>1882</u>
        1   + 3 + (19) (10) 1 = 5 BIRTH NUMBER

5th: Add Name Number to Birth: 5 + 6 = 11 = 2 REALITY
                                                NUMBER

6th: Add the month and day of birth to current year:
       January 30 added to 1933
         1   3   (16) 7 = 11 = 2 PERSONAL YEAR
                                               NUMBER

NOTE: 1933 carries the same vibration for him as his REAL-
ITY NUMBER, making it a very important and vital year in
his life. It is a turning point, depending upon the use he
makes of the finer, spiritual qualities given him by his REAL-
ITY NUMBER.

The numbers 11 and 22 always add a spiritual force to any
name or position in which they are found and give possibility of mastership in handling human affairs.

These six divisions of the name represent a definite, clear-
cut method of character analysis and may be used for this
purpose, for they give a key to the individuality and character likely to be expressed independently of the REALITY
NUMBER. Each division has its own meaning and takes
its part in building up the talents, inclinations, abilities, interests and experiences which form and shape human
destiny. These are often so marked and dominant that the
REALITY influence may be lost track of or submerged and
neglected until it is too late to work with it, so that the latter
days of life are inactive, dependent and idle. The fullness of
life which should crown every individual is lost somewhere

in the past because of this failure or lack of recognition of the true self.

Therefore, it is very important that the REALITY indications should be more carefully studied than any other number or position of the name and its possibilities be recognized with the others, otherwise life may not bring the soul satisfaction that it seems to offer when youth looks forward to the future. For, after all, the REALITY represents the essence of experience and not the processes by which experience is gained.

In reading the character from the above points: the HEART NUMBER shows the desires, ambitions, longings, likes, dislikes and personal concepts which are deep in the heart of the individual. It shows how you feel about things in general and what you desire for yourself.

The PERSONALITY NUMBER shows the outer expression, the manner and personality. It is the way you appear to others or your approach to people.

The DESTINY NUMBER is where the work is to be done and shows the conditions to be met and worked with in order to get on in the world. Your name shows why you were born, what you were named to do in the world and the kind of experiences you will meet, but it does not show the final outcome of your life. The REALITY NUMBER shows this. The DESTINY is where you work, and the REALITY is what you worked for when all has been accomplished.

The BIRTH NUMBER is the foundation upon which you stand. It is what we draw upon to fulfill our destiny. It represents the tools of the trade and natural talents. These are blended into the REALITY through the ideals of the heart and activities in the field of opportunity or destiny.

The PERSONAL YEAR NUMBER indicates the method to be used and the experiences to be gained during that given period of time. The activities of the PERSONAL YEAR change from year to year. But the essence of the experiences colors the future, and if properly expressed, helps toward success.

You express your character through the above divisions of name and birth and you may meet your real experiences through any person, condition or activity which carries your number—family, husband, wife, children, relatives, house number, business address, phone, car, day, month or year—for numbers appear at every turn of life, and it is the wise man who reads the signs and indications of experience. The following relationships will help you understand your attraction towards others and help you to find your own.

THREE

Reality Relationships

REALITY AND HEART NUMBERS

When your REALITY NUMBER is the same as the HEART NUMBER of another person, that is, when the vowels of another's name add up to the same number as your REALITY NUMBER, a deep and interesting attraction will be felt by each of you. This attraction may bring about a lifelong friendship, and a mutual interest may be developed, especially by the one having the HEART NUMBER.

From the first, there seems to be an understanding, and a warm tie may be cemented which will last even after a separation. The circumstance of the attraction is often unusual or peculiar—even taking on a romantic color. In some cases, a strange antipathy may be felt, similar to that which is found when two people dislike each other at first, then fall in love, simply because the attraction is so deep.

It often happens that the person having the REALITY NUMBER at HEART may be attracted to you before you are to him or her, or at least may be conscious of the attraction first. Your appeal to this person is to the inner nature, and as the acquaintance ripens, your character will be developed and rounded out by the ideals and opinions imparted to you from the depths of the other's heart. In many cases, this individual gives more in the way of unselfish friendship than you do, but seems to enjoy doing so. But as you unfold your own ideals under this giving, you in turn give something of yourself which is pleasing to this friend, and a perfect balance of giving and receiving is established for your mutual benefit.

Much progress can be made through this relationship, for this is more than an ordinary acquaintance. It is not for material gain; instead, it is the pathway of the soul.

REALITY AND PERSONALITY

This attraction is not as deep or as lasting as that of the HEART. But two people are often drawn together because of something in the manner or appearance of one or the other which appeals to their tastes and fancies. When a closer association is entered into, disappointment or unhappiness generally result, because there really was no foundation or similarity of character upon which to base a relationship.

The PERSONALITY represents the appearance, manner and outer expression and does not reveal the deeper states of mind or the real quality of character. Those who have your REALITY NUMBER as their PERSONALITY NUMBER may attract your attention and interest because of their looks, the way they dress or express themselves in the social activities in which you meet them. They may seem to be your ideal. But this fancy should not be taken too seriously, for it may not mean happiness for you. A man may see something attractive in the PERSONALITY of a woman and fall in love with her because she represents in her manner what he is developing through the demands of his REALITY NUMBER, only to find that he was misled by appearances and that she does not have the character to satisfy his developing nature. Or a woman may meet a man in the same way, deceived by appearances, and find that he is not the true mate.

All attractions based upon the pull of REALITY NUMBER to the PERSONALITY of another offer social interests and may be a stimulant to your mentality or challenge you to a better presentation of your own PERSONALITY. But generally such acquaintances will teach you that it is not wise to judge from appearances and to look beneath the surface in human relationships.

REALITY AND DESTINY

Much benefit can be realized through this association if it is rightfully understood, although the attraction may not be of a deep or lasting nature.

When a person has your REALITY NUMBER as a DESTINY NUMBER, a vague desire to take part in his activities, enterprises and social activities or to enter his field of endeavor will be stirred in your mind, for your REAL SELF will sense there is something there which will give you a chance to expand or gain a personal benefit.

There may be little understanding or appreciation of character by either of you, for this association has more to do with worldly activities than with the urge of the soul. Such a relationship is not often carried beyond an experience which teaches a lesson, sometimes easily forgotten by the DESTINY, but leaving a mark upon you. For you will have had an opportunity to develop your character, even though hardly recognizable at the time.

Often this relationship may not go beyond a social or business contact. The DESTINY person developing his opportunities finds in you an interest or inspiration or something he can use as a stepping-stone. But his worldly activities may cause him to break the tie, often without real regret, as he goes on to new fields of endeavor. However, it is a fifty-fifty contract, for even though you may help him do something he wants to do, you will find that through doing this you have developed your own character and gained wisdom that will be an advantage to you later on.

Now and then unhappy experiences result from this sort of attraction. Each may make use of the other to further his or her own ends without giving exchange. Deep feelings can be stirred up, jealousies aroused and a strong dislike felt underneath a manner of friendliness. If the REALITY person is not aware of what may be gained by the association, he or she may covet what the DESTINY person has or seems to be doing and can cause trouble from this desire. But it is the REALITY who must have the self-control and make the effort to learn the lesson which must be gained. In the DESTINY he is meeting an outside condition which is forcing him back upon himself and developing his own character. He must give something of himself in return for the lesson he is learning, for it is only when there is a real desire to improve the self that the exchange of experience is of value to either. The DESTINY gains a better expression, and the REALITY finds himself and develops his talents and abilities.

REALITY AND BIRTH

When an attraction is felt between the REALITY, and a BIRTH or a tie is found which links the two together, it is of an important nature, very deep and having to do with past incarnations. The ideas and abilities are similar, through training or interest in previous lifetimes, and the association comes about through causes set up in other lives. Therefore, the tie is a subtle one, due to deeper forces than are apparent on the surface.

An important work may be accomplished in this lifetime and useful attainment may be worked out together if the effort is made. But the tie may not be fully harmonious, even though love seems to be there, for the relationship is one of a balancing nature in which a test is undertaken and a spiritual debt paid.

The BIRTH individual will often find the greater test in the association because he is apt to be fixed and positive in the characteristics of the BIRTH NUMBER, while the REALITY person is unfolding his characteristics. Often the BIRTH NUMBER has to sustain and uphold the REALITY and take part in his mental and spiritual growth, even to the point of forcing the REALITY to develop and grow whether he wants to or not. This may cause suffering, pain, dislike, resistance and even sorrow, for the REALITY meets a strict teacher in the BIRTH but must conform to his requirements, and the BIRTH finds a difficult student in the REALITY.

Should the REALITY take all the BIRTH has to give and be indifferent to what the BIRTH is doing for him, there may be retribution later and the REALITY be forced to repay and repay in order to gain his freedom. This tie can be a very binding one and hard to break, unless a real effort is made by each one to understand the other and to compromise for the good of both.

So when you meet someone who has your REALITY NUMBER on their BIRTH, look out for a deep experience, for the attraction may be the bait which leads you to your fate and a needed lesson.

REALITY AND REALITY

As the REALITY shows the development to be made during a lifetime, two people with the *same* REALITY NUMBER will feel an interesting attraction and realize that they have much in common, because both are going in the same direction on the highway of life.

This is an attraction which can result in much good and leave its mark upon the character of each, for they can support each other in the experiences they are taking for growth and development, even if they are seemingly of very different natures. This tie may be unusual, out of the ordinary, with no binding tie or demand upon each other beyond the mutual sharing and the pleasure they find in being with someone of their own type or interests.

The tie may last a lifetime if the lessons demanded of each are gained at the same rate of unfoldment. However, it is not uncommon to find the relationship broken up, no matter how strong the tie may be, if spiritual development is not equal. And sometimes, too, circumstances brought about by different destinies may lead them apart, even though the purpose they serve is similar.

REALITY and REALITY working in common can lead to splendid results—to sympathy and satisfaction not experienced by other ties in life.

REALITY AND PERSONAL YEAR

Each year of life brings its special opportunity and requirement. Change is the watchword of progress, and although one is born for a special destiny, each year brings a force to be met and used for future growth and development. We climb up the ladder of life step by step, and the personal year represents the step one must take at this time to make real progress.

When you meet your REALITY in your personal year, the experience taking place during this year will be very vital and have more influence upon your future than any year during the cycle, no matter how important other years may seem to be. Therefore, every effort should be made to take advantage of this opportunity—it is a time to go forward in the direction of the work indicated by the REALITY NUMBER.

REALITY AND PINNACLE

There are four important cycles of experience to be lived through during your lifetime. These are called the Pinnacles of Attainment. They operate independently of character, showing the avenue of expression, the field of activity and the path to be traveled while the character is being developed.

If your REALITY NUMBER appears on one of these pinnacles, that cycle will be the most important for you and your future, for during that time you will have the opportunity to work along the lines of your REALITY and to succeed through its activities.

If your REALITY NUMBER does not appear on any pinnacle, your REALITY development will take place more generally. It may be late in life before its full power is realized.

The pinnacles are found as follows:

    1st Pinnacle: Add month and day of birth together.
    2nd Pinnacle: Add day and year of birth together.
    3rd Pinnacle: Add these two sums together.
    4th Pinnacle: Add month and year together.

The 1st Pinnacle operates between the time of birth and the age found by subtracting the birth number from the given number 36.

The 2nd Pinnacle operates during the next nine years.

The 3rd Pinnacle operates during the next nine years.

The 4th Pinnacle operates during the rest of the life.

EXAMPLE:

       January   30,   1882
          1 +   3 + 1   = 5 Birth Number

    1st Pinnacle: 1 + 3 = 4
    2nd Pinnacle: 3 + 1 = 4
    3rd Pinnacle: 4 + 4 = 8
    4th Pinnacle: 1 + 1 = 2

36 minus 5 = 31 . . . . time of 1st Pinnacle
31 plus   9 = 40 . . . . time of 2nd Pinnacle
40 plus   9 = 49 . . . . time of 3rd Pinnacle
49 to end of life . . . . time of 4th Pinnacle

Mr. Roosevelt was under the 1st pinnacle until he was 31 years of age (36 – 5 = 31); the 2nd Pinnacle until 40 years of age (31 + 9 = 40); the 3rd Pinnacle until 49 years of age (40 + 9 = 49); and the 4th Pinnacle for the rest of his life (which is his REALITY number). His best period of life appears after 49 years of age and gives him his greatest opportunity to express his highest quality of mind and thought.

REALITY AND CHALLENGE

There is a challenge against one's success hidden deep in ever character. This is apt to act unexpectedly or when least desired, no matter how clever or skillful the individual may seem to be. Even the unfoldment of the REALITY and the highest opportunities of life may be defeated unless this challenge is met and corrected.

The challenge acts in a peculiar way, for it is not something to overcome but something to *become* and use. When a more perfect expression of this quality of thought is gained, a happier use of the talents is the result.

If your REALITY is the same as the challenge, you will meet many obstacles in accomplishing your REALITY, or seem to suffer until you strengthen or correct the indicated weakness. If another person has your REALITY number for a challenge, you will meet a very big test through that person's peculiar expression and character. The challenge is found by subtraction as follows:

$$\begin{array}{ccc} \text{January} & 30, & 1882 \\ 1 & 3 & 1 \\ \hline & & \\ & 2 \ - \ 2 & \\ \hline \end{array}$$

0 CHALLENGE

1st: Subtract the month and day.

2nd: Subtract the day and year.

Then subtract these two remainders from each other. This is the CHALLENGE and is present during the lifetime. Do not subtract a cipher from a number—when a cipher appears during the first or second subtraction, it represents a more difficult period, especially during the time of the cipher, which is half the lifetime. When a cipher appears as a full challenge, the individual must make his life what he wants it to be and not depend on others or circumstances. The cipher is a big challenge, but generally means a universal opportunity due to the soul's choice and selection, based on an inherent capacity brought over from other lifetimes. Other numbers represent a challenge according to their meaning. In a few cases, a fourth number is found on the challenge by subtracting the month and year. This acts during the latter days of life.

Franklin Delano Roosevelt has a CIPHER CHALLENGE, which indicates that he has an opportunity for a big life—but also a big challenge. He has met a very deep test in life. But the cipher is not his REALITY NUMBER. He must meet his challenge in other ways as well, for the cipher has no limit.

FOUR

Reality Numbers

Numbers are symbols of character and experience. They never change their meanings. A number appearing on a house or street has the same meaning as when it appears on destiny or birth, but will be interpreted according to the position in which it is found, representing experience for house or street, and character and opportunity for name and birth. All numbers are good and never express their qualities negatively. It is only the conflicting relationships into which they are forced by the activities of everyday experience that bring negative expressions. If an individual seems to be expressing a number negatively, this may be due to the presence of too many of the same numbers in the arrangement of name and birth, giving too great an intesity of that particular quality for harmony or success. Or again, a number may be in combination with another number in such a manner as to be unable to be true to its own expression. The saying, "things are at sixes and sevens," is a good example of this.

During the first part of your life you may seem to be a combination of the positive and negative forces of the number, especially if you have no knowledge of what your REALITY NUMBER is. Later in life you will notice that you are most consistently the expression of the positive characteristics of the number, and if you have been fortunate enough to train these qualities from youth, you should be well established in life and satisfied with what you are doing in the world. And even though you have not consciously cultivated your REALITY talents, you will find them present to some degree in your expression of character. Whether you wish it or not, your REALITY influences and colors your individuality.

The following delineations may be applied to numbers wherever they are found, but are more especially intended for interpretation of the REALITY NUMBER:

NUMBER ONE REALITIES

Life is seldom dull for these people, for they have strong powers of attraction and are unconsciously drawn into interesting and often peculiar experiences.

Their greatest success comes through new places, new things, new situations and also through original and unique ideas. They get better results from starting new things than from taking over old lines of work. Often they do well by undertaking undeveloped projects, which give outlets for their individuality and leadership, as they are not naturally the type to follow others or take subordinate positions.

Leadership is often thrust upon them early in life, and they should always stand for what seems to be best for themselves, although eccentricity or peculiarity of temperament should be avoided. Their individuality should be harmonious and helpful to others. When a number one REALITY finds eccentricity or disharmony of character developing, every effort should be made to correct this, for the ultimate success and position of the latter days of life depend upon constructive ideas. Any extreme only brings unpopularity and regret.

Strong opinions and ambitious natures enable them to become leaders and directors of others, holding positions of authority if they desire. But they should guard against a tendency to boss or dominate, and show fairness in all dealings, for egotism or self-importance brings jealousy and personal resentment to mar their success.

A necessary course of action is dignity of manner, and it is best for them not to become too familiar with friends and associates, for most of their unhappy experiences result from too close intimacy with others.

When their individuality is negatively expressed, they can act in a very annoying manner by separating themselves from others or refusing to do as others do, always wanting to do something different. They may deeply resent direction, refusing to do anything they are directly told to do, and can be extremely contrary. They often ask advice but never follow it, for they have their own strong convictions and are seldom influenced by the opinions of others. If very undeveloped, they cannot see anything beyond their own desires, disregarding others, and are very conscious of their own importance.

Well developed individuals have a broad vision and are capable of carrying out plans on a large scale. They have a magnetic force which, if used spiritually, brings illumination and inspiration to all who touch their lives. They like to accomplish what they have in mind and are never long without some idea or plan. They generally take immediate action when the plan is clearly in mind. They have good memories, fine powers of concentration, which help them get what they want, and in vital moments something always turns up to help them. This makes them appear to be self-centered, and they often are, although they cannot be called selfish, for they grant others the right to have what they want. They are simply people of a single purpose with a deep-seated desire to maintain their individuality, which is necessary for them, as their success comes through following their own ideas and creating their own pathway in life. For this reason, happy self-development must be their constant endeavor. In fact, if they accept too much advice they are apt to lose their way in life and fail to reach their goal. Without a plan they may become vacillating and careless and have to constantly fight for their rights, so it is best for them to have a plan and work it out, although it may be of an extreme and unusual nature. This cultivates their courage and ideals and eventually takes them to the head of some undertaking or interesting work in which they find their true place in life and fulfill their destiny.

There is generally some peculiar quality of sensitiveness which characterizes these people. They will be very strict about something. This could be order, law, obedience, or in regard to children and love affairs. They are capable of deep affection, but are really people of one love—one man/one woman—even though they may marry more than once. They are not really conventional, but do not purposely break conventions; they simply do things differently without forethought and in their own way. They have few real friends because of decided likes and dislikes, and can defeat their own happiness by clinging too closely to old friends and old attractions. When they do so, some unhappy experience generally affects their home, forcing them to let go and stand on their own feet.

Health is one of their problems, to keep well one of their tasks. They have fine powers of recuperation but should never over-estimate their strength. Money is generally fair; at least when there is a real need for it, it is always found and help will be given in an emergency. An active life is necessary, for this brings to them the right people and opens up the opportunities which are so important to their success.

They succeed as originators, inventors, promoters, engineers, designers, executives, heads of departments, overseers and in all lines of endeavor where qualities of originality and force are essential.

NUMBER TWO REALITIES

An ability to get what they want without doing things themselves is one of their characteristics. They gain through association and easily attract those who will help and sustain them. Their fine powers of diplomacy, ability to smooth out difficulties and get on well with others enable them to influence people, even though they are not the true executives. They win their way in life with ease and success, especially when they understand their own inherent powers. They are great lovers of peace and do not quarrel readily—generally getting results as harmoniously as possible—but when driven too far, will fight for their peace. Their pleasing and appealing manner, adaptability, charm of personality, tact and agreeableness make others want to please them. They are also endowed with a spiritual grace, which enables them to become healers and comforters to mankind and a light to the world. "BLESSED ARE THE PEACEMAKERS, FOR THEY SHALL BE CALLED THE CHILDREN OF GOD" is their motto. This is especially so when the two comes through the number eleven.

When their abilities for doing good in the world are not harmoniously expressed, they can go to extremes or lose their power to help others through an over-intensity of feeling, especially along the lines of religion, politics or food. They can even become extremists with no middle ground regarding principles or standards of living—at times outspoken in speech, which is rather surprising from those so naturally refined, cultured and esthetic in feeling and mood.

A natural senstitivity is the source of many of their negative qualities, and unless rightly understood and directed, may cause them much suffering. But it gives them charm of manner, gracious personality, deep feeling and sympathetic understanding of others, and their sincerity of purpose shows when they are happily expressing their talents.

This sensitivity also gives self-consiousness, a dread of meeting people, shrinking from the opinions of others, fear of what others may think, and it is possible for them to develop an inferiority complex and live in acute self-depreciation, which can result in illness and disappointment. This is due to a psychic and intuitive sense wrongly used, for their natural psychic powers and intuition are some of their finest assets when rightly expressed, giving them the ability to make use of and understand the subjective forces of being.

They readily respond to love and tenderness and require the same sympathy and patience for their own development which they give to others, for their sincerity of nature gives them the desire to do the right thing, to please others and to share what they have. Co-operation is the fundamental law of their lives.

When TWO REALITIES find themselves expressing things negatively, they should cultivate a sense of humor, laugh at their fears and live in faith, for it is faith, not fear, which makes them "rulers over men." Their true success and happiness is not found through fighting things but by establishing harmony and agreement in the conditions in which they find themselves. This is done by making a greater effort to express the beauty, tenderness, sincerity and spirituality of their natures. Trouble in partnerships or associations is not an uncommon experience during the first part of their lives, and up to about forty years of age this may be the test they cannot escape until they realize the true helpfulness of their characters.

A talent for music is present and they are especially fitted for some line of artistic expression, if not in a professional way, at least for their own satisfaction. If this talent is neglected, it brings regret later in life. This talent may be voice, dancing, violin, literature or painting. They can also lecture, teach, make splendid orators or speakers, quite often are interested in politics and diplomacy, arbitration, and in being ambassadors. They succeed in the ministry, medicine and spiritual healing, and are successful as treasurers, tellers, paymasters, accountants, secretaries, and in all acitvities dealing with money, banking and finance. Radio and higher mechanics, electricity and statistics, often attract them. They are also found as club workers, in societies, fraternities and organizations, for they like to join others and be a part of what they are doing.

Nerves and head are sensitive parts; good health depends upon the state of the nervous system.

NUMBER THREE REALITIES

Imagination, inspiration and emotion are the true expression of the THREE REALITIES. No matter how practical the character may be, due to other numbers in the name, some avenue of expression along the more creative, fanciful and artistic lines of interest permits their true growth and development. At some time during their career there will be an urge to speak or write, and eventually life will force them to make use of their natural gift of words. Imagination and ability to talk well are also a part of their business success.

There often seems to be a repression during the first part of life, interfering with ease of self-expression and use of the imagination and talent. This repression should be weeded out and every effort made to follow an artistic career. This may be literature, drama, or commercial or mechanical art, depending upon the other numbers in name and birth. But not to be allowed to use the natural gifts of imagination and creative ideas may mean lack of health and an unsuccessful life. The early repression in life may be a difficulty in enunciation or may be simply a retiring nature, as all THREE REALITIES are extremely sensitive about what is said to them. Many a three career has been given up because of what someone said about them. In the training of children, or even when helping an adult, care must be taken not to cause self-consciousness through carelessly spoken criticism, for this can be felt so keenly that they will make no further effort, even refusing to explain or give any reason why. The sensitivity of the THREE REALTIES is about themselves, while the sensitivity of the TWOs is quite different and concerns people, conditions and circumstances.

Underneath the cheerful and agreeable nature of the three there is a strong feeling of self-importance, which if allowed to rule their character may become a negative quality, but when rightly used becomes a very vital power in their lives and often carries them to great heights of attainment. It enables them to accomplish deeds of valor, to carry out spectacular and glowing undertakings and to do great work in a worthwhile way. It is the threes who give color to life, who amuse, thrill and inspire. Were it not for their daring vision and imagination, the world would be commonplace and uninteresting.

The THREE REALITIES have a natural urge to be obliging and at times can be generous to a fault, even to the point of sacrifice. They will give freely and love to protect the helpless. As long as they can have their own way and things run smoothly they are the nicest people in the world, but when not pleased they may show a surprising indifference to others—even be a little touchy, refusing to do what does not please them. Even an adult can show some of these childish traits of character. They should cultivate a more positive expression in defeat and realize that they are often very selfish, even with their usual obliging and kindly nature.

At times they may seem to be easy-going and lack firmness of will, but this is not so, for they are really very self-determined, holding on to a plan or possession like grim death, even to the point of losing friendship and business.

Their fine creative powers and imagination win things for them in a business way in spite of personal faults, for they do things easily and unusually well when left to their own resources. They can be very successful and have the gift of vision, prophecy and the ability to make dreams come true. They are the most unhappy people in the world when not properly placed and can have a very hard life and no money until they find their true self-expression or activity. They should enter public life, for both men and women learn by public experience. They often think they do not want the limelight but really enjoy it when it is turned upon them.

They are good in music, singing, designing, dramatic art, color, decorating and in all lines of amusement and entertainment. They compose, write, teach, lecture and are more fond of opera than jazz when true to their higher nature. Stocks and bonds interest them and give opportunity; also real estate and property. They are sometimes boxers, fighters, great warriors and soldiers, for they fight at the drop of a hat—or at least have a snappy comeback for their enemies. They generally have a philosophy of life which helps them to the top, for they are naturally cheerful and optimistic people. They deal with the essence of things; have mediumistic tendencies; often are too impatient to work with the practical but can be very particular regarding detail. When not happy, they become worriers, see only their side of the question, and may be extravagant in thought and action. They are honest but may be careless and forget to pay what they owe. Friendship means everything to them and they make lovely, sincere, lasting friends. They are often sacrificed by friends, and many unhappy experiences come through love affairs and family. They make interesting companions, have a capacity for enjoyment, appreciate beauty and luxury and generally attract these things to themselves. They are not physically strong but have good recuperative powers and make lots of money when doing the right thing in the world.

NUMBER FOUR REALITIES

Builders, constructors and natural organizers, it is their duty to bring ideas and plans to concrete form and to establish order in all undertakings. This may be along scientific, artistic, religious or business lines, according to other numbers in the name. But the bigger things in life are gained only as they make dreams practical. During the early part of life, even up to the thirty-fifth or fortieth year of life, this may not be fully realized or accepted as true to character. But close observation reveals that they are struggling or yearning to put some idea into concrete form, and that they love to manage, organize and shape material when given the chance to be true to their own ideals.

Later in life they develop a splendid talent for organization, born of this early struggle, and they may be found in large, worthwhile projects which have a permanent and lasting purpose. They are hard workers, like to keep busy, and are generally at the head of the work to which they are giving their time, for they uphold and maintain order, system and routine and establish the permanent order of things. They are not natural originators, but when the idea has been presented they have a clever way of getting things done, even on large scale, sometimes building systems and establishments which last long after their part of the work is done.

They may be found in activities which have to do with buying and selling, administration, public utilities, agencies, soliciting, hiring, employment, regulation of ceremonies and in the practical management of any well-established business. They often succeed through educational matters, promote campaigns involving educational work, and are drawn to activities having to do with documents, papers, contracts, examinations, law affairs, lending and exchange of property and real estate. Many storekeepers dealing in commodities, fixing things and supplying the practical needs of daily life are found among FOUR REALITIES. Commercial art and religious affairs give them opportunity also.

Time is essential to the ultimate success of whatever they are building or planning. Activities which require patience, perseverance, steadfast determination and which grow slowly give them the best results. Haste and impulse are apt to be their undoing; therefore, they should build for a sure and lasting future. They grow through responsibility, hard knocks and their own mistakes. The easy pathways of life should be avoided by FOUR REALITIES. Effort brings out their strong qualities of courage, high standards, sense of values, honesty, concentration, application and deep good nature, which are the keynotes to their success. They are tireless in their efforts to do the right thing; very exact and patient in detail, they are not likely to be carried away by fancy or imagination, although much emotion may be otherwise shown by the name, for the practical side usually dominates and controls their actions. Now and then they can be too exacting and a little dominant, for they like to have their say and are anxious at all times about what is right. They like to give orders rather than take them, and expect others to do the right thing in the same way they do. For this reason they are often found in their own business or where they are in full charge, as they are often severe, not easy bosses, and too sure their way is the right way. They are kind and truly helpful in spirit and may be greatly admired and respected for the fine work they do, but not always deeply loved because of this severe side to the nature which appears when an order is given or a rule is established.

The negative side of their characters may be expressed in a sort of know-it-all manner, and they can become chronic fixers, telling others what to do in a superior manner and refusing to take the blame for their own mistakes or to be told anything about their faults. Undeveloped FOUR REALITIES are unable to learn, due to stubbornness and a contrary spirit deep in the nature.

But FOUR REALITIES must be given credit for the splendid work they do and the foundations they place for others to stand upon. They govern themselves by strong principles and discipline their own actions with the same severity and exactness they demand of others. They do not waste time or material. They will even sacrifice pleasure for work. They are never idle and drive themselves as well as others in their efforts to get things done well and according to schedule. When they use their energy along constructive lines and meet the obstacles which stand in their way, they have a wonderful ability to energize everything they touch and to take their place in the world of lasting progress. When their efforts are built upon the rock of endeavor and not upon the shifting sands of emotion, they build for a certainty and success which is never lost.

One of the big problems met by FOUR REALITIES is to free themselves from the condition which holds them down. This is very often family ties or family interference. They must get out into life, build by their own endeavor and work with their own tools, even though limited in the beginning, until by perseverance and experience the foundation is placed for expansion and greater success. Those who adapt themselves to conditions and circumstances placed by others may live a carefree life but not a happy one. To settle down to a life of routine through marriage or family ties which is not in some way created by their own efforts gives the possibility of becoming narrow in vision and thought and of learning little from life's school to build character. Some who are held down from not knowing how to free themselves and who have never tried to build a world of their own may become very resentful, moody and ill when suddenly forced to meet the struggle of life. When they do fight for their rights in a constructive way, quietly and skillfully working out their own ideas, or taking up a study which expresses their true individuality, they are capable of overcoming the seemingly impossible and of climbing past the last barrier which holds them down.

FOUR REALITIES are not really fond of social life or the worldly phases of expression. They are not good mixers and prefer a few good friends having similar interests. They may be active in a business way but retire to the quiet of the home when the work is done. They sometimes work too hard and should remember "all work and no play" is not the best method for health and progress. To cultivate enthusiasm is often the cure for failure in the lives of too-serious FOURS.

Their steadfastness, patience, endurance and fine understanding of facts give them the power to control the world, for were it not for their abilities to dig deep and make secure, there would be but little permanency in life.

Good health depends upon self-control, exercise and common sense in eating, otherwise stomach troubles, high blood pressure and heart disease develop.

NUMBER FIVE REALITIES

These people are of independent spirit and belong to all public activities. They are resourceful, versatile, alert to opportunity, and color any environment in which they find themselves with their enthusiasm. They bring speed, new life and action to any undertaking and are usually clever in turning failure into success through their quick wit. They are rapid thinkers, quick to grasp new ideas. They make changes easily, have fertile minds, highly charged imaginations, and the gift of languages and smooth-flowing words, which may work to their detriment as well as to their success.

If given the opportunity to travel or make changes, they do so easily, for monotony is death to them and they find it hard to remain a long time in the same place or to permanently associate themselves with routine endeavor or dull home life. An inner restlessness causes them constantly to seek change, for there is an undying urge within their souls for a fuller, more abundant life and personal freedom. If they do not have the opportunity for this or are forced to accept a regular settled routine method of living, they can become very unhappy, restless, impatient, critical and show extremes of feeling, even becoming eccentric and seeming to lack the necessary application to make a success of life. They are often accused of lacking in application, because they do not stick to things very long at a time, but this accusation generally comes from those who do not understand their clever energetic natures, for if given the right to be free, they often accomplish much more than the routine plodders.

They are interested in many things and like to know what is going on in the world. They are curious about life and not afraid to have experiences. They find their best opportunity through fluctuating activity and where their love of variety and resourcefulness can find outlets. They find stimulation through people in general and lose their power if not frequently given active and exciting interest through which to express their abundant energies.

There is a social side to their natures, and their many experiences, wit and personal magnetism make them very good companions. They attract the opposite sex and have many worldly experiences, often among unconventional people. A peculiar characteristic about them, however, is that even though they are freedom-loving and independent, they are great sticklers for the law and are often found working in legal professions or activities which formulate and control the legal rights of the people. Their ability to act quickly on important matters makes them leaders of movements and progressive affairs in which the majority are interested. They become the heads of organizations and companies, not because they are really executives, but due to their abilities to keep things moving forward. They are not creators or originators but they stimulate activity and are able to get a lot out of others because of the zest they put into things.

They are bold and invincible when aroused to action, and are even aggressive when challenged by a real obstacle; they will go to the limit to get results. It is often very hard to say no to FIVE REALITIES when they demand yes, and they can be very unreasonable when personal ambitions or interests are at stake. When negative in expression, they can have a don't-care attitude regarding the feelings of others. Even the most evolved may show a bit of boastfulness when pleased by personal accomplishments. The negative fives accept without thought what others do for them and fail to recognize the cost or sacrifice others have made to help them, also failing to give credit where credit is due. All FIVE REALITIES seem to get a big thrill out of life.

FIVE REALITIES have more extremes of temperament than any of the other numbers. They can be so fine and wonderful, but also astonishingly difficult and unkind. A destructive side of character gives them the desire to tear things down, to destroy and cause trouble, born of their inner restlessness and discontent. They can be very analytical, unsympathetic, sarcastic, critical in speech and manner, and in public life can stir up rebellion in governmental and political affairs. But this is due to the misdirection of their progressive spirit, which is the actuating force of their thought. If this is expressed constructively, they become public benefactors, wise counsellors and bring progress and new life to the common people. Their analysis and criticism is then turned to research and scientific study, and they become the most charitable, tolerant and enlightened people in the world.

Opportunity comes to these people through change and new things, but change should only be undertaken after they have mastered what they have been doing, so that some degree of skill can be given to their work. Too strong a desire for freedom and too many adventures will give little that is permanent or lasting. The value should be extracted from each experience mentally, emotionally and spiritually. And there should always be a headquarters or place of rest where they keep the tools of their trade, for after all, the "rolling stone gathers no moss," even if it does become smooth from much rolling.

Opportunity in business is found as newspaper reporters, columnists and story writers. All fields of publicity, advertisement and travel give them successful results. They succeed as lawyers, politicians and government officials. The fields of amusement, sports and entertainment interest them. They make splendid salesmen and can sell anything from a pair of silk stockings to a new religion. They do well in clothing, regulating styles, and in commercial art. Fives are often found in speculation and promotion, but gambling will bring ruin in its wake, for the law of change always operates in the money affairs of FIVE REALITIES. The occult, the mysterious and the unusual hold an interest for them, and while they are not deep students, their cleverness enables them to look ahead and seize opportunity while others are dreaming about it. These people bring progress to the world, and without them the world would grow stagnant and dull.

Health depends upon right living; illness is brought about through nervous conditions, intestinal and liver trouble.

NUMBER SIX REALITIES

Affairs of the heart, love, home, marriage and humanity greatly influence the lives of all SIX REALITIES. Family, parents, relatives and children mean a great deal to them, for they are strongly idealistic, romantic and affectionate. They live on a very high plane of life when true to their higher natures, and have strong principles ingrained from childhood about religion, families, right and wrong. They demand truth, justice and fairness for all and from all, and are conventional in thought, wholesome, honest and forthright. They are lovers of peace and harmony and seek to bring these qualities to all their undertakings. They need harmonious conditions in order to do their best work. They have a fine sense of duty and service but are apt to go to extremes in fulfilling a duty or sacrifice themselves foolishly for some ideal or person, for they like to be useful and do worthwhile things in the world. In fact, they are most unhappy when not in service to humanity or following some ideal. When their talents are brought to constructive use, they generally become the humanitarians of the world.

They are lovers of the home, desiring its perfection and beauty, and make splendid fathers and mothers, careful and wise in the training of family and children. Later in life they become cosmic fathers and mothers due to their humanitarian tendencies, and take part in the training, care and protection of down-trodden humanity. They are dependable in marriage and very indulgent with those they love, almost too much so, for they can be absolutely blind to the faults of loved ones. Even though doing public work, they need the protection of home and family, being dependent upon the love, approval and sympathy of others. They live on a very idealistic level of thought and require sympathetic understanding in order to do their best.

Many unmarried men and women are found having the SIX REALITY. This is because they cling too tenaciously to ideals and hold the marriage state so high, or they feel they cannot meet the marriage responsibilities the way they should be met, according to their dreams. Some are unmarried because of family disagreement or tragedy, and now and then the spirit of sacrifice, which is so strong in their characters, causes them to give up what they desire for the sake of one they love. Sometimes love comes late in life to these people as the reward for their service, and it is often more beautiful than an earlier love affair. Their ideals are very fixed and beautiful, but they are capable of a great deal of unreasonableness, even stubbornness, when their opinions and ideals are challenged by others. They do not like to have their methods interfered with and can defend themselves if criticized or condemned.

Even though they are the great humanitarians and influence the hearts of humanity, they seem to have a personal side which keeps them from realizing any imperfection in themselves, for there is a great deal of sentiment and personal emotion mixed in with their service and helpfulness.

They are always very generous; over-giving is one of their chief faults. They are apt to be too charitable, or give foolishly where it is not needed, just because they feel the desire to do so, and then fail to recognize the real need of those they are helping or loving. Then again, they may be spasmodic in giving, giving abundantly today and failing utterly to give tomorrow when it is expected. They may beggar themselves in a foolish way for charity and be unkind to loved ones or sacrifice family for some outside interest because of an over-exaggerated ideal of service, much like the mother who speaks at the welfare meetings while her own children are on the street improperly cared for. It is this strange contradiction of character which brings them difficulties and what they call lack of appreciation until through experience and their own mistakes they learn to strike a balance between giving and receiving.

But they really have the gift of service in a worthwhile way and the ability to be helpful to others without thought of return, when living true to their highest possibilities. They live in dreams, dislike the sordid and do much to make life beautiful and sweet. But they do not compromise or give up their ideals, and if they cannot do what they want to do, they will not do anything. They want to give all they have in the way they desire, as it is a sort of "love me, love my dog" principle, which is sometimes hard for the other person to accept. They often live in a world of unreality and feel a perfect satisfaction in what they know and are doing, and unless they are careful can become self-righteous. ("The King can do no wrong.")

Sometimes they have the habit of telling others what is wrong with them, based on their love of truth and justice, and they can be very blunt, outspoken and almost too frank in their remarks. They cannot take their own medicine in this respect, and if undeveloped and not making use of the great love and charity of their natures in some constructive manner, they can be narrow, fuss over little things and be foolishly strict in demanding obedience. This tendency is generally corrected when they feel they are loved and understood, for they grow, improve and radiate beauty when they are given love and sympathy. They overcome their faults more easily through sympathetic cooperation than through criticism or strict demands on the part of others. Like the FOURS, they do not like to be hurried and require time to find themselves and their usefulness.

They have a good earning capacity and fine financial attraction. Often they make fortunes or gain through marriage and inheritance. They should be able to surround themselves with luxury and comfort, which they greatly appreciate, without hard work and by their natural ability, for they are not physical workers. If they find they are drudging or laboring for money, they are not doing the right thing for success.

They are very artistic and can make money through artistic lines of work and through activities which have to do with the luxuries of life. They like an abundance of all good things and are successful in work which provides these things for others. They make good cooks and chefs; even the men like to fuss around the kitchen and take part in domestic activities.

Music, flowers, gardening, pottery, furniture, interior decorating, all lines of commercial art are vocational possibilities. They are often singers or actors and make good story-tellers, poets and painters. They are fine teachers and can take care of and educate children. They make splendid nurses and physicians, and all health methods give them opportunities for service and money. They succeed through welfare work, institutions, hospitals, hotels, apartment houses and restaurants. They also make good lawyers, farmers, ranchers and succeed through horticulture and livestock. Irrigation, boats and ships attract them, and many are engineers and miners. They are sometimes called lazy, for they make money easily and without much effort when they are doing the right thing.

They have strong religious tendencies; many become reformers, even though they are orthodox in thought. They cannot stand hard conditions and the heart and circulation need to be carefully watched when health is not good.

These are wonderful people—they help humanity find the beauty of life. They are always helpful and comforting when trouble knocks at another's door.

NUMBER SEVEN REALITIES

Outstanding and unusual characters, they occupy a place in the world all their own. They are separatists and live their lives in their own way, apart even in the midst of the crowd, reserved, refined, dignified and very hard to understand. They often misunderstand themselves and feel unrelated to the everyday activities of life. They may desire to join with friends in the worlds of excitement but do not find their real interest there. Life itself often forces them to stand alone, calm, serene, depending on nothing but their own soul's grace.

They seem to be a law unto themselves and do not find their success in the ordinary activities of the world or through people, situations or conditions, but through inner knowledge, soul realization and higher understanding. They seem to be compelled to master circumstances and to adapt conditions to their own level of understanding. They must be

the thinkers, students and knowers of the world and discover the principles of life, get to the facts of existence. They
are developers and discoverers and reveal the hidden laws
of being. They seem to deal with cold facts and hard knowledge but are really dreamers and visionaries, looking to the
realities of the unseen for power and success rather than to
the material facts of established conditions.

They are not adaptable people and have a great deal of
pride and reserve of manner. They do not like to mix with
everyone and are often hard for others to meet or talk to;
they seem to keep their thoughts to themselves, seldom ex-
plaining unless they wish to do so. They are extremely
averse to being asked questions, even though they frequently demand exact explanations from others. They are natural
doubters and skeptics, especially if undeveloped, and they
must have facts, demanding the right to think out their own
problems in their own way, for they are not satisfied until
they settle the question in their own minds. They work best
alone or from behind the scenes and need periods of repose
and meditation. To be forced to live in constant confusion
and activity causes them to lose their power of attraction,
takes away their skill and ability to command their own
peculiar success in the world.

In many respects they are natural stoics, capable of marvelous self-control on all planes of being, and the wiser ones
learn early in life that their power is in poise and repose.
When they allow emotion to rule, it has a way of ruining
them and stripping them of all power. Introspective and
thoughtful, they should take all their problems into the quiet
places within their own souls before acting upon them, for
as they neutralize passion and desire and make them consis-
tent with the facts of higher laws, their affairs are carried forward to a better level of power and understanding. They are
often very quiet, silent and reserved, especially if they have
lived a repressed life, not making use of the finer inner
power of mind and brain. But when they understand these
qualities and appreciate them, and do not try to be like

others, they can be good-natured, pleasing, charming people, developing an appealing personality and commanding the interest and attention of everyone they meet.

They are splendid talkers if they desire to be and often become convincing and compelling speakers, as they do not lack for words when upon familiar grounds. When not interested, it is very hard to get them to talk, which heads to the impression that they are limited in this way, but it is more often sensitiveness and lack of familiarity that holds them back. They need to have faith and confidence in those they deal with before they reveal their true selves. Even though reserved, they are not lacking in feeling and are often more affectionate and loving than they appear to be. They are naturally "untouchables," and frequently build up a wall which cannot be broken down by anyone they do not like. They are capable of living an esthetic life—of withdrawing from the world in order to escape the so-called common things of life—and can live a solitary existence when interested in some spiritual or mental line of thought or research. They have very little real interest in foolish or frivolous things and seek knowledge above all else. The more evolved SEVEN REALITIES would rather read or study than eat, and with all their self-control and coolness of head, they are capable of being carried away be some idea or principle which appeals to their sentiments. There is an exactness to their natures; they like to get the truth of everything. They do not like to waste time on nonessentials and are capable of understanding the fine points of the law. They like to have a plan well in mind from beginning to end before accepting it, demand the best in all things and have a fine appreciation of value and class. A woman furnishing a house will have the vision in mind down to the finest details, and may shop for days to get some detail just right or to make the proper relationship. They like to get full value for what they give and are sometimes considered a little close. They do not spend extravagantly, but will pay for the best if they want it. They are not the philanthropists of the race but will give to a worthy cause if appealed to.

Their possiblities are tremendous through research, calculation and analysis. They should endeavor to excel in some special line of work, for they do not belong to the general workers. They are specialists, having the power of synthesis as well as analysis. Intuition and soul power color the activities of their minds. They are scientists, investigators, inventors, historians, chemists, technicians and find interest in laboratory and statistical work. They succeed in insurance, in mathematical lines of business and make excellent lawyers and surgeons because of their cool nerve and strong willpower. They deal successfully with books and literature and make fine detectives, criminologists and secret service men, for they like to uncover the hidden and the unusual, helped by fine intuition and unexpected "hunches." They have mystical qualities, may be interested in occult and spiritual matters, and often become the heads of secret societies or schools of an occult nature. When their power and ability to discover hidden facts are made use of in a constructive way, they generally become famous and make a name for themselves presenting some new principle or scientific accomplishment to the world.

They are artistic, too, often connoisseurs in the realms of art and music. Scientific art interests them and they work well with their hands, frequently developing skills in carving, etchings and the use of finer tools and instruments. They also make good educators and health specialists. An important consideration for the developing SEVEN REALITIES is a good education along specialized lines. Generally it is wise to leave them to their own resources to find their own occupation in life, as they do not fit readily into the places occupied by others and can fail utterly if forced into work which they do not care for.

Marriage is something of a problem for them, due to the silent and reserved part of their nature and the strict attitude of mind which characterizes their more serious interests in life. They love a good home, well furnished, elegant in style, but they do not like it filled with too many people. They expect to be the head of the house and far too often fail to express the love and tenderness in their hearts which is necessary to make it happy. They should not be too exclusive in manner or interest and should keep in touch with the world, for too much study can make them dull and cause them to lose opportunities in life.

Health is gained through a specialized diet, periods of rest and care of the glands, spleen and eyesight.

NUMBER EIGHT REALITIES

These people have more need of understanding themselves than any of the other numbers, and few fully realize their power. Mastery on all planes of being is their possibility and also their requirement. Life's rewards must be earned, for the gifts of money and ease may be suddenly taken away unless ambition and desire are colored by character and worthwhile accomplishments. They must learn to strike a balance between the spiritual and material forces of life, as unusual opportunity is given them from on high for success in any undertaking. When they strike this balance, power, authority and recognition crown their lives, for they are reapers and garner what they sow.

Strong characters, capable leaders of men, eights find that the rewards of life are not easily attained. They are destined to work for a purpose, to try and reach a goal of efficiency, to direct the minds of humanity to a higher attainment and to give their all to whatever they undertake. To think only of money and commercial power is to court failure and downfall, from which it is difficult for them to recover, not being on the money level of endeavor. Money comes to them through efficiency, knowledge and good judgment, but they do not have the easy money attraction of the threes and sixes, for money is a reward of work well done and not a privilege to be coveted or expected as a natural right.

Their natural tendencies are philosophical and psychological, for they like to theorize and examine the reasons for things. They are clever in relating feelings and facts and are able to understand life in its totality—looking into life as it really is, without illusions or prejudices.

When awakened and developed, they demonstrate their mastery by working for the cause of humanity, not in sacrifice, but from pure love of the work itself, asking no personal credit but the satisfaction of having done good work. Their reward is the accomplishment.

Repeated effort and much mental strain are always part of their undertakings, as the momentum of life forces them to be strong. If one of these people falls from grace by taking the easy pathway, the whole chain of life is weakened. They gather up the reins of life, direct the work of all the other numbers and organize life's finer forces, often without full appreciation, because none of the other numbers have the same power to regulate, control and direct so efficiently.

The number eight which characterizes their experience is often called karma and the death of material hopes. But this is only so when there is no real purpose in life, or when the energies are spent striving for wealth and personal power; then the will is broken by life's tremendous force, for eight is the number of mental attainment and the ability to do things on a large scale.

There is a constant struggle felt by EIGHT REALITIES to hold life at an even keel, as the two loops of the number typify two levels of life, the higher and lower, or heaven and earth. Like the tides of the sea, the affairs of their lives are constantly changing, and if the environment of life is easy and comfortable, with little required of them to succeed, a warning is present, for unless effort is made to use their gifts for some worthwhile purpose, the foundations upon which they stand may be washed away and be very hard to regain. But if the tide is out, and the lower level of life is experienced, repeated effort and steady aim for some higher purpose will eventually lift them up to a reward for work well done; even then, life may not be easy, for constant effort is necessary to maintain the balance between the higher and lower, and efficiency is the ever-present need.

Through this mental struggle, an inner power is developed, and their cool, unprejudiced management of affairs enables them to rise to an emergency with so much power and force that they become outstanding characters in their community and nation.

The number eight is often considered a money number, but there is no real attraction for easy money in the lives of EIGHT REALITIES. They handle money well and often become splendid businessmen and women, but financial success is generaly due to the power they assert for the good of the many rather than to any real financial attraction. They earn money fast and let it go as fast as they earn it, although they are careful about the use of it in their personal affairs. They seem to be attracted to money but can be very impractical and at times seem to have no real money sense. They can handle money for concerns and companies, being very trustworthy, but for themselves they may be "penny wise and pound foolish"—for after all, they are more interested in what they can get for it than in money itself. However, when they learn wise judgment and make good use of their mental powers they never lack for necessary compensation.

They are natural instructors, overseers, supervisors and coaches, capable of helping others to success. They find opportunity through literary work, publishing, printing, newspapers and business syndicates. They are good correspondents, travelers and explorers; they make good mountain climbers or may be born near the mountains. They do things in an unusual way and have more courage than the average individual. They are unusually good in governmental positions or where they can superintend and control others and they always have people under them, being better at the head of things than in subordinate positions. They are civil engineers, efficiency experts, superintendents, insurance agents, architects and have ability in the intelligence service and statistical departments. Sometimes musical ability is shown, and careers in the professional arts and sciences are common. They are splendid nurses, are able to control the insane and have great power over animals. They love nature and the wide-open spaces and succeed through sports, games and entertainment; also through hotels and summer resorts, especially those in the country.

Their health is not all that it should be, for they use so much nervous energy that it is liable to bring on nervous indigestion, but they have marvelous powers of recuperation and often live long lives. They are not good marriage companions or the best sweethearts, for even though they have a deep love nature and are loyal and true, they are too self-sufficient and do not spend much time in foolish sentiment. They should marry someone they can admire or look up to, and the mate should be equally strong and capable in order to insure complete happiness. They are usually attracted to those who have special talents or mental attainments. They can reason coolly about what they are feeling and this puts the damper on real romance. They should live in the country for health's sake and keep a balance between physical and mental activities. EIGHT REALITIES have good style and forceful personalities but when negative can put up a good bluff and be somewhat showy in method, going to make a good appearance.

All EIGHT REALITIES should hold positions of authority among those who are educating and building a race consciousness. They do not appear as humanitarians but are teachers of the race. If they live up to their ability to understand the higher and divine law, making it of value in material affairs, they can become great masters and mystics, and the world will seek them out for their understanding.

NUMBER NINE REALITIES

To express the Brotherhood of man, to have power and compassion and to be all things to all people, are the keynotes to happiness for NINE REALITIES. They must be bigger than all others and all conditions in life and must grow from the personal into the impersonal to reach their goal. Otherwise they can suffer and be torn to pieces by life's conflicting experiences. It is often hard for NINE

REALITIES to understand the importance of this, for their opportunities are so large, so all-embracing, that the gifts of life
seem to be handed to them on a silver platter. But in order
to keep these gifts, they must give up the things of the flesh
for the things of the Spirit, and all personal ideas must be
dissolved in the universal consciousness. This may be a
painful process, for while the consciousness of a great love
pervades their souls, human love and emotion hold their
heart. The contest between the two brings their greatest experience. They meet broad opportunities, as they have
cosmic protection, and the affairs of their lives move in large
circles. But as they are finishing a cycle in incarnation, making ready to go on to greater achievements in future lives,
they are compelled to keep the law of higher things if they
wish their reward.

They have tremendous power of feeling, of such high
voltage that it can light the world and warm the heart of
humanity when it is poured forth without personal motive
or desire. But when it is turned upon themselves for personal gain and satisfaction it can be like an explosion of
dynamite, wrecking their lives and destroying their power.
They must love much, wisely and well, but to desire love for
personal satisfaction alone leads them through a soul
crucifixion of a deep and trying nature. To cling to personal
things too tenaciously is to lose all, but when they look to
the universal, not to people, for joy and happiness, they
receive greater love than they ever dreamed of, both per-
sonally and impersonally.

This is the number of reward, and to be impersonal and
broadminded places them in command of the greatest good
in life.

Soul growth is their keynote, and to let go of self opens the
way to a life of power, commanding position, service, divine
realization and understanding. When this is gained, they become the chosen people of the earth.

The demand life makes upon them to be all things to all people brings them many experiences. Because they are kind,

generous, impulsively take on the responsibilities of others, sympathetically seek to help the weak, the old and the poor, giving without reserve, even to the point of weakening those they serve, they are frequently imposed upon by others. But eventually life forces them through disappointments to realize the truth of giving and to take an impersonal attitude; then they learn to help and serve others without losing the responsibilities of their own growth and development. Strange experiences in love, marriage and friendship serve also to show them the truth—that sacrifice is not the pathway to true love. True, they must give and give, but without thought of self, for when the personal enters, pain follows.

Early in life, while gaining their own realization, the personal and impersonal run side by side in their characters and they may seem to be very inconsistent. They will give to an extreme and be very tolerant and patient at one time, then very suddenly become cold and detached, keeping their affairs and money to themselves, but this is generally when they have been imposed upon. So it is well not to drive the number nine too far, for none can be so extremely hard and difficult when the limit of endurance has been reached, or love wounded.

They are idealistic; unless they can idealize in love, home and work they turn quickly to some new ideal. Because they are romantic, emotional and idealistic, they fall in love with great intensity, but the romance will end just as suddenly if they do not find the ideal or the higher and finer expression of love. They simply cannot stand people or conditions which offend their ideals of beauty and loveliness, and they have something to learn in the way of tolerance and charitableness, even though they are the lovers of the world.

They are esthetic, impressionable, imaginative and have very high standards of beauty and perfection. They may even go to excess in their desire to reach this perfection, but after many disappointments and experiences, they learn to look to principles and not to people for the perfection they seek and know exists.

Some ot the NINE REALITIES are very timid and shy and not at all aggressive. They often require a helping hand until they realize their tremendous power to attract every good and perfect gift through love and service.

When undeveloped, they can be meek and vacillating, looking on the dark side of things, turning from one thing to another, searching vainly for the beautiful things in life, not knowing that they must produce them by their own inner power and grace. When they encounter temptation they can fall very low and be very mean and small. But none of the other numbers have such a marvelous power to restore position and rise from the bottom to the greatest height and remain there. They are difficult to change or reform when developing wrong habits but are capable of the highest in life when they make the effort to overcome their faults.

Their keen sense of perfection makes them dislike common things, and they have a great contempt for small actions in others. They have a horror of unlovely things, poverty and old age, and may go to extremes in feeling and action because of this. They live in a world of dreams, colored with beauty and grandeur, but this enables them to create beautiful things and is the source of their vocational power and success.

They can turn virtually nothing into something beautiful and attractive, taking seemingly worthless articles and making them beautiful and worthwhile. They bring charm to everything they touch. They have a fine attraction for money and wealth and do not care to do menial work. They have a very creative vision and generally attempt big things. They should never lower their standards, for they can reconstruct and rebuild human lives, if they desire, and take part in the civilizing of humanity along the emotional and imaginative side of life. They make splendid teachers, fine surgeons and lawyers, due to their ability to improve civilization on a broad scale and because of their desire to help others find a better and larger life. They are very artistic and dramatic and wonderfully clever in putting people in the right places in life. They are writers, story-tellers, actors, actresses and can succeed through plays and theatres. They are fond of color and can do original work in color through painting and designing. They often think up original things in practical art, and find interests in upholstering, cabinet-making and architecture. They want the best in life in food and surroundings and have a splendid power of attraction for the comforts of life. They make fine orators, speakers, and talkers and use their imagination to make life interesting. Religious, philanthropic and charitable activities interest them.

Nine fathers are very important in family life, and children are very close to their hearts. Their health is generally good, but their endurance is not great, as deep emotion and feeling are hard on their health. They should always take time to keep well.

To be redeemed out of all creeds, dogmas and beliefs into the one life in all and through all means victory for the NINE REALITIES.